Speaking *of* History

THE INTERLOCUTORS

ROMILA THAPAR is emeritus professor of history at Jawaharlal Nehru University, New Delhi. She is a Fellow of the British Academy and holds an Hon D.Litt each from University of Calcutta, University of Oxford and the University of Chicago. In 2008, Thapar was awarded the prestigious Kluge Prize of the US Library of Congress. She has authored over 25 books.

NAMIT ARORA is a writer, social critic, and the author of three previous books, including *Indians* and *The Lottery of Birth*. Trained in science and technology, he has spent over three decades educating himself in the humanities, history and other social sciences. His recent work of public history is a ten-part web series, *Indians: A Brief History of a Civilization*.

Speaking *of* History

Conversations about India's Past and Present

Romila Thapar
Namit Arora

Three Essays
COLLECTIVE

Published by Three Essays Collective
First Edition November 2025

ISBN 978-93-83968-47-3

This paperback edition published by Three Essays Collective is authorized for sale worldwide—except in the Indian subcontinent. A different hardback edition (identical contents) published by Penguin Random House India is authorized for sale exclusively in the Indian subcontinent.

Three Essays
COLLECTIVE

Three Essays Collective
B-957 Palam Vihar, Gurugram (Haryana) 122 017 India
Tel: +91 98681 26587, +91 98683 44843
info@threeessays.com; Website: www.threeessays.com

Contents

Preface

by Romila Thapar

The idea for this conversation arose after a spontaneous discussion I had with Namit Arora about why history is so misunderstood in some circles. So, we decided to have an extended conversation to clarify the salient points and see where it might lead.

We begin with how the past was represented in premodern India, the role colonial scholars played in crafting its early historical narratives and its impact on the subsequent construction of Indian history. Colonial histories were partially accepted and partially challenged by Indian nationalist historians. Not having to see history through the colonial lens—and the use of a new and wider range of sources and questions—led to a certain freedom in exploring earlier periods. It also brought the study of history into the orbit of the social sciences, enabling a deeper and richer understanding of the past.

This shift led to professional historians being required to use the acknowledged historical method—a systematic approach to evaluating the credibility of evidence and constructing a logical, causal understanding of past events. This method made the writing of history significantly more authentic and reliable. By the late twentieth century, professional historians were expected to be well versed in this approach. Their training included proficiency in analysing historical sources, such as reading primary texts in original languages, understanding the nature of archaeological and epigraphical evidence, and incorporating insights from related disciplines such as anthropology, linguistics and sociology.

Some histories have been written to highlight select events. Many civilizations, for instance, were portrayed as having had a 'golden age'—framed as the unique expression of a civilization's genius. Today, however, historians understand civilizations not as isolated, self-contained entities but as products of continuous interaction among diverse cultures. The emphasis has shifted towards tracing these interconnections and exploring how cultural exchange, adaptation and synthesis have shaped historical development.

There also emerged at this time an awareness of what came to be called historiography, or the study of how history is written, by whom it's written and under what influences. While historians study the past, their thinking is also conditioned to varying extents by their times and experiences. These influences may affect their reading of the past, although the thoughtful historian is aware of this problem and tries to minimize it.

In the writing of Indian history, many with no formal training as historians have nonetheless written books claiming to represent India's past. These works often include fantasies and mythological events, presenting an idyllic vision of the past—when life was supposedly peaceful, harmonious and more virtuous than the present. Such narratives, lacking the critical analysis of sources that professional historians employ, contributed to the rise of what are sometimes called fake or pseudo-historians: writers who fabricate or embellish the past and then insist that their versions are historically accurate.

It is difficult to assign a single label to such authors. Some of us refer to them as 'popular historians' and to their work as 'popular history'. But above all, the allusion here is to the quality of their work, where they often act as propagandists and narrative peddlers, crafting seductive stories that distort the past to serve present agendas.

However, not all non-academic writers of history fall into this category. A few have taken the time to familiarize themselves with the historical method, undertaken impressive research, engaged thoughtfully with the work of academic historians and written worthwhile history. Their work often has broad appeal and is considered part of what we call 'public history'. Academic historians take these individuals—public historians—seriously and recognize the merit of their work. Unfortunately, their efforts are often overshadowed by the abundance of misleading narratives that dilute public understanding of the past.

These conversations are an attempt to explain how historical research has evolved and how it has affected the reading of Indian history. They seek to distinguish between academic historians and the self-styled popular writers who, lacking rigorous methodology, often peddle misleading narratives that foster confusion and inflame social tensions. While it's important to recognize that historical interpretations can change with new sources or a fresh understanding of the problem, the reference here is not to the differences between contending schools of academic history. What we have explored here, among other things, is the problem that arises when academic historians have to contend with non-historians writing a fantasy history.

Our conversations have also been most enjoyable for me, and at times have opened up new perspectives. I have also benefitted from Namit's gallantry in taking on the more arduous work of shepherding the book through its many phases.

Introduction

by Namit Arora

Last summer, Professor Thapar and I found ourselves discussing the dismal state of popular history in India, marked by evidence-free assertions, a deep suspicion of academic historians, and its troubling infiltration into school textbooks. Amid interruptions from Bulleh, her adorable dog, who insisted on his share of attention, we reflected on the causes and forces behind these distortions of history. We exchanged some thoughts on why history remains so poorly understood even among college-educated Indians, despite its deep influence on our beliefs, values and collective identities.

On my way home, a thought struck me: Wouldn't it be fascinating to explore Prof. Thapar's historical insights at some length, especially for a non-specialist audience? How does Prof. Thapar see the origins and evolution of historical scholarship in India? What does she think of colonial history and its continuing effects on our sense of the past? How might she describe the 'historical method' that historians use to validate, analyse and interpret historical sources? And since history, like other social sciences, is not as objective as the physical sciences, how should readers assess the reliability of a historical narrative?

The questions kept multiplying in my mind! I imagined discussing some of the most contentious topics of Indian history, spanning caste, gender, migration, invasion, violence, nationalism and more. What propels the Hindutva view of history? How should academic historians respond to its distortions in the public sphere? Amid all its absurd and inflated claims about the Hindu past, what aspects of actual Hindu culture does Prof. Thapar consider pride-worthy? She has described herself as an 'old-fashioned Indian nationalist', but what does that mean to her? Does she see herself as the 'Marxist historian' that many claim she is? And what are some of her favourite works of the imagination from early India?

After mulling it over for a few days, I proposed the idea of a conversation to Prof. Thapar and was overjoyed when she agreed. She suggested we discuss why history has become so controversial in recent decades but left it to me to figure out the questions and additional topics. I emailed her a set of 'starter questions' to anchor our discussion. Our conversation then unfolded organically over two immersive evenings in her living room, with follow-up exchanges in subsequent meetings and over email.

Once transcribed, we edited the text for clarity and flow. Though it retains the tone of a casual exchange, some elements—verbal tics, emphases, tonal shifts and non-verbal cues such as nods, gestures and smiles—were inevitably lost. However, through this editorial process, the dialogue gained readability and depth, additional arguments and examples. Somewhere en route, we decided to publish it as a small book.

§

It may surprise some to learn that Prof. Thapar has often said, 'As a historian, I'm not searching for "the truth". I believe we'll never fully uncover the truth about the past because the past is gone, and we cannot return to it.' Instead, she sees the historian's task as that of explaining the past—and its relation to the present—by relying on the most credible sources and rigorous analysis. Her aim is not to discover absolute truths but to construct a reasoned, evidence-based interpretation of what likely happened, why and how. These interpretations are inevitably shaped by subjectivity, but they aim for greater explanatory power than competing narratives, at least for those who share similar criteria of truth and ethics.

This is now a baseline view in the study of history worldwide. When historians investigate a historical question by sifting through primary and secondary sources, examine their multiple viewpoints and uncover hidden layers, the notion of a single, definitive 'truth' proves elusive. Even when working with the same materials, historians may interpret them differently based on their frameworks, values and assumptions. So we end up with multiple, sometimes conflicting, accounts of the same event. That's not a flaw. It's a feature of serious historical inquiry—as long as those accounts are grounded in reliable methods and a transparent, critical reading of the evidence—as we explore in our conversations.

This is also why history must remain open to a diverse community of scholars—diverse in social background and thought—who are committed to pursuing fresh evidence and sound reasoning. One way to overcome the blind spots or biases of individual historians is to read widely across a range of scholars. A more inclusive academic environment is also more likely to ask bold new questions, challenge inherited wisdom and reject arguments based solely on authority. While far from perfect, this scholarly enterprise, with its many self-corrective mechanisms, is the most reliable way we have yet found for advancing knowledge in the social sciences. Contrast this with other efforts—such as Hindutva, Islamist and Zionist accounts of the past—that masquerade as history but disregard its methods. These 'histories' routinely put the cart of ethnocentric interpretation before the horse of dubious facts and are fuelled by elementary and motivated misreadings of sources.

§

These conversations also explore history's evolution as a discipline in colonial and independent India. From the mid-twentieth century, academic history began drawing on insights from sociology, economics, anthropology, psychology and other related disciplines. New methods and perspectives collided with traditionalist academia, which still saw history as mostly political chronologies of kings and empires. Against this backdrop, a new generation of Indian historians—D.D. Kosambi, R.S. Sharma, Ranajit Guha, Bipan Chandra, Irfan Habib, Romila Thapar, K.N. Panikkar, Sumit Sarkar, Harbans Mukhia, D.N. Jha, Uma Chakravarti (all born before 1942) and others—began introducing new research methods and innovative courses in Indian universities. This included social and economic histories, which examined, for instance, the interplay of social relations, economic systems, caste, gender and political power, producing more vivid insights into the lives and times of our ancestors.

This crop of historians also challenged long-standing Eurocentric and colonial narratives. These included the portrayal of India as a static and despotic society; the periodization of Indian history along religio-ethnic lines; the oddly persistent belief that Indian culture began only with the Indo–Aryans and the Vedas; and Marx's ill-conceived idea of an 'Asiatic mode of production'. They also critiqued the orientalist construction of modern Hinduism, shaped by their overreliance on textual sources and Brahmanical elites.

New intellectual developments such as postmodernism raised scepticism in the idea of history as a source of objective truth. This has led to many debates, including the curious case of some postmodernists labelling Prof. Thapar an 'old-fashioned empirical positivist'—suggesting that she subscribes to the notion of objective historical knowledge, untainted by personal biases or the social values of her age. But this view seems to me unfair. Although Prof. Thapar does not herself identify with postmodernism, her work has come to exhibit at least a few of its traits. These include attention to subjectivity, social context, identity and power relations in analysing the past. As these conversations also illustrate, she has blended such insights with a secular, evidence-based historical method, which has proven intellectually robust and highly productive in her scholarship. Consider, for instance, her book *Somanatha: The Many Voices of a History*, where she examines how social memory is often shaped independently of the historical record, revealing the complex interplay between memory, storytelling and power.

A newer generation of scholars is now building on all of this foundational work, advancing sociocultural history by looking at India's past through more focused lenses—such as caste, tribe, gender, faith, sexuality and now genetics. They are exploring new histories of inequality, ecological ideas, trade, migration, language, science and technology, economic and fiscal systems, 'the early modern' and more. Scholars from subaltern, Ambedkarite, adivasi, transgender and other long-marginalized groups are asking bold new questions 'from below', using fresh data, new analytical methods and alternative readings of extant sources. They're examining how the dynamics of power and knowledge—including in the writing of history and its undue focus on elite groups and their perspectives—has shaped Indian society.

Prof. Thapar has remained intellectually engaged with these developments. 'All knowledge has to be questioned,' she has often said—and no historian's interpretations should be set in stone. This is precisely as it should be. What matters most is that the writing of history and its evolution should be guided by the empirical–rational spirit of the historical method—which we discuss at length—the closest thing in history to a gold standard for reliable scholarship.

§

We both felt that a handful of complementary images would make the book more visually engaging. Prof. Thapar suggested that we look beyond the usual repertoire of classical sculptures and paintings, which already receive ample attention. Instead, she proposed highlighting art forms less familiar in mainstream culture, such as adivasi and Tantric art. These forms are rooted in distinct social values, imaginations and aesthetic sensibilities, often diverging from those of dominant groups. Yet, they've significantly shaped Indian culture, even if only subconsciously for many of us.

This shift opened up a rich array of possibilities. Our final selections were shaped by our personal tastes, what we felt an artwork signified, and pragmatic matters such as the availability of high-quality images and rights. Though most artworks are contemporary, we believe that they retain ties to the past, quietly echoing historical themes through their motifs and symbols. These images—better in colour but impressive even in black and white—are not intended to illustrate the text but to remind us that there are many artistic and cultural worlds beyond the ones we most often see.

By design, this is a selective exploration of India's past and present, with greater emphasis on Prof. Thapar's area of expertise: ancient and early medieval India, exemplified in her classic *The Penguin History of Early India: From the Origins to AD 1300*. The choice of the topics was largely mine, and I often wished we had time to cover many more. Readers expecting the sweep of a general history textbook or the depth of a specialized monograph may be disappointed. What we set out to create instead was the texture of a living-room conversation—frank, probing and centred on a few key issues—rather than a 'balanced' historical survey. My hope is that it sparks curiosity and encourages readers to embark on their own wide-ranging readings and conversations.

When our views diverged—whether owing to my insufficient knowledge or reflection, our different assumptions, a generational difference in outlook or other reasons—Prof. Thapar responded with patient reasoning, pointing to alternative interpretations, urging greater nuance, openness, critical inquiry and reliance on wider evidence.

These conversations were deeply absorbing and enriching to me, and in our effort to make complex ideas more accessible yet intellectually satisfying, they also became a shared learning experience. We invite you, dear reader, to listen in and reflect on what makes history reliable—and why that reliability matters.

These dialogues reveal our respective approaches to historical questions, but we hope they will also offer new ways for you to think about the past and the world around us.

1

The Beginnings of Historical Scholarship on India

NAMIT ARORA: Prof. Thapar, let's start by reflecting on the role and impact of history in our lives. It was mainly in the modern period, two or three centuries ago, that history emerged as a subject of secular and critical enquiry. Historians began using rational and empirical methods inspired by science to investigate new questions about the past and the origins of societies. They began providing fresh accounts of the rise and fall of cultures, civilizations and nations.

This new kind of 'rational knowledge' and its production turned into an influential scholarly enterprise. It began forging new ideas of the self and new collective identities, shaping both nationalist movements and globalizing projects in recent centuries. It is hardly an exaggeration to say that historians have dramatically altered our sense of who we are, as individuals and as peoples. I think that in modern societies, professional history's impact on our lives and times is way more profound than we often realize.

In India too, scholarly history, or history as critical knowledge, began during the colonial period. What was its early trajectory and how did it shape Indian self-knowledge over time? For example, let's imagine some early eighteenth-century Indian elites and the state of their historical knowledge—how they imagined their past, social origins, etc. How has the modern discipline of history changed that understanding and to what effect?

ROMILA THAPAR: Yes, that's a fundamental question, but I would go further back than the eighteenth century. I would argue that this obsession with knowing about the past has long captivated people in every society. It leads us to ask questions such as, how and where did it all begin, who started it, what happened after that and so on. Initially, this is the raw material of mythology. It takes the form of an explanation, but it's mostly made up of what you *like to think* may have happened. And that's a fundamental distinction between mythology and history. The former is what you believe *might have* happened because you like what you build as fantasy. The latter is much more demanding because history is based on proving that something happened, and then explaining why and how this happened, and basing this explanation on logic and reasoning. With mythology, none of these matters. You go on embroidering the myth to suit new human needs and fancies.

There has been a very long tradition of mythology in India. Every community, every social group, every caste has its own mythology about its origins, the past, how it all began and so on. So that's how most eighteenth-century elites likely saw things. However, some of those who were in power and had authority, such as royal dynasties, had already been organizing their past in genealogies and chronicles, reflecting elements of a historical sensibility. But only in the last couple of centuries have some more Indian communities been putting the past together more systematically and asking historical questions.

During the early period of colonialism in India, in the late eighteenth–early nineteenth century or so, the colonizers asked a question of the colonized: What is your history and where is it written? And the Indian response was: What do you mean by history? We can tell you how we represent our past, but is this what you're looking for as history? By this time, Europe was introducing rational–logical methods of investigating the past. So what its scholars and thinkers looked for in India was knowledge produced by such analytical methods. What they mostly found was mythology but also some small degree of more reliable history.

For Indians, the past and its events are summed up in the word used for history, *itihasa,* or 'this is how it was'. This was a mix of causal explanations and stories with some attempt to give them authenticity by linking them to the concerns of the community that composed them. Later, it gradually began to include narratives that drew on a degree of historicity—as for example in the royal historical biographies and in the chronicles of the ruling dynasties. *Harshacharita*, the biography of King Harshavardhana, is an example of historical biography; Kalhana's *Rajatarangini* and Barani's *Tarikh-i-Firoz Shahi* are examples of the chronicle. This was somewhat the pattern in some other societies too as they slowly began to recognize the difference between myth and history.

Evidence is the key idea that shifted the discussion of the past away from mythology towards history. Without colonialism, the trajectory of historical inquiry in India would likely have been quite different. It might have remained largely within the realm of mythology until, with wider social changes, new approaches and understandings of various aspects of culture eventually took root. Modern methods would have arrived but perhaps more slowly.

The early Indian approach was not always regarded as a reflection of actual events, though this assumption could occasionally be revised or questioned. Such accounts may be better understood as imaginative representations of the past, rather than attempts to reconstruct what truly happened. Nevertheless, we must remember that even historical narratives which claim to describe real events often contain an element of imaginative representation.

So, in the late eighteenth–early nineteenth century, colonial power assumed that Indians had no written history and that they would have to create it. They set about discovering the Indian past and constructing it into what we call colonial history. This is where the writing of people like James Mill (1773–1836) becomes crucial.

NAMIT: Especially the religion-centric periodization that Mill imposed on Indian history, dividing it into Hindu, Muslim and British (Christian) periods—determined by the religion/ethnicity of the most powerful rulers in these periods.

ROMILA: Right. This is an early strand of colonial history. Mill proposed that India's past had to be studied in terms of these two religious communities, which he refers to as two nations: Hindu and Muslim. But he was wrong, as they were not nations. He attributed to these highly diverse socio–religious communities a perpetual, permanent hostility towards each other, which is his own invention. The communities as nations are his invention, as is the hostility. This becomes the bedrock of colonial history, which begins with the theory of there being two nations defined by religion in constant conflict.

NAMIT: I suppose Mill's characterization was heavily shaped by the long history of conflict between Christians and Muslims in Western Eurasia—such as the Crusades, the Reconquista, the fall of Constantinople, etc.—and so he was determined to apply a similar template to the Indian past, whether or not it was similarly valid here. And he wrote his influential history of India without ever visiting the subcontinent!

ROMILA: Yes, and then there was a second strand of colonial interpretation. It had emerged a bit earlier from William Jones (1746–1794) finding linguistic parallels between languages such as Sanskrit, Old Iranian and Greek, implying some possible nascent connections or perhaps even common origins. A few decades later, in the nineteenth century, Max Muller's study of the Vedic texts suggested these as the root of Indo-Aryan language and culture. Soon, Europeans were discussing the possible origins of Aryans outside India, while the idea of their origins within India appealed more to the Theosophists and some others in India. It began to be said that the origins of Indians and their religion and their culture may be traced to the Aryans and the Vedas. But what was the identity based on, language or race? The origins, nature and impact of the Indo-Aryan people have sparked a long-standing and often contentious debate, shaped by both scholars and non-scholars. This is sometimes referred to as 'the Aryan question'.

The third strand relates to the different framing of history itself, as in Europe versus Asia. Against a dynamic cultural history for Europe, colonial historians saw the history of Asia as one of oriental despotism. It was interpreted as a static society with no history, no evidence of change, no state system. The ruler was a despot, and through a bureaucracy he controlled the peasants who provided the labour and produced the wealth for the despot. Oriental despotism was assumed to be the normal pattern for Asia. So influential was this idea that Karl Marx's concept of the 'the Asiatic mode of production' was based on it.

By the end of the nineteenth century, we have these three strands, these three stories about the Indian past. By the early twentieth century, the theory of Oriental Despotism largely faded out because it was challenged and shown to be untenable, but the first two theories continued. What role did they play?

The Aryan theory became fundamental to explaining the origins of people, of social divisions in societies and the beginnings of the religious beliefs of Hinduism. Brahmanical texts were highly respected by the Indian elite, so colonial historians treated them as primary sources that mirrored the society of their time, ignoring the specific perspective from which they were written. Not only were some of the Brahmanical prejudices incorporated in the construction of the Indian past based on what these sources said, but their statements and descriptions were taken as reflecting the entire Indian society.

This was not something unique to the Brahmanical sources. Authors of such texts often reflect their own approach to social matters and historians therefore should not assume that they reflect the thinking and behaviour of the entire society. They have to be seen as limited to that section of society to which the author belongs, unless the author clarifies the opinion it represents. The historian therefore has to always inquire into the social and personal background of the author whose text is being quoted.

The politically important aspect of Mill's *History of British India* (1817), virtually the earliest colonial history of India, is that his theory became the root of communal thinking. Mill saw all Indian history in terms of Hindu and Muslim communities. The Muslims arriving on the scene were viewed as coming solely as invaders and, therefore, antagonistic. That becomes important to the creation of attitudes towards the Other.

The point I'm making is that much of this early historical writing about India reflected a distinctly colonial view of the past. In the last fifty to sixty years, Hindu groups—especially those aligned with Hindutva—have, whether consciously or not, absorbed this framework. Even without naming Mill, they have implicitly relied on his theory as a foundational lens for understanding Indian history. There are others who oppose the theory and disown it as history, describing it as a fantasy of colonial writing about the Indian past. While it may not be entirely fantasy, it is largely so, and it must be questioned. That's one of the issues on which currently there is contestation.

NAMIT: So the earliest historical writing on India—moving beyond sporadic biographies and dynastic chronicles to attempt a critical analysis and explanation of the past—emerged in a colonial context. In these works, the view of our past was tainted not only by the colonizers' prejudices and uncritical reading of Brahmanical texts but also by their asymmetric power and domination. European elites had come to espouse some rather simplistic and self-serving ideas of 'civilization' and 'progress'. They needed them for self-justification of their 'civilizing' mission, and its often violent pursuit of profits and other ends over means (a world view that Indian elites later incorporated within their own idea of 'development'). Colonial-era historians were thoroughly implicated in this colonial project, as scholars like Edward Said and more recently, Priya Satia, have shown.

It's now widely accepted that in order to portray their own rule as full of virtue and light, colonial historians characterized the preceding centuries as one of relentless misrule, religious conflict and darkness. Early nineteenth-century Hindu nationalists were only too happy to accept the British Indologists' caricature of Indo–Muslim rule. This strikes me as a clear example, among many others, of enduring mental colonization on the Hindu right.

But, alongside the three tainted strands you've outlined, weren't there also other British-led efforts that were remarkably productive and insightful, like the deciphering of Brahmi, the discovery of our Buddhist antiquity and the Harappan civilization, their work on translations, and much else that greatly and positively expanded our historical imagination?

ROMILA: Exploration of the Indian past by British and other European scholars did reveal a much fuller past, a more complex past—in other words, a past that is intellectually exciting to unravel. Studies of ancient languages constituted the discipline of philology, the deciphering of ancient scripts came into the purview of epigraphy, and excavating and recovering the material remains of the past happened through archaeology. People were used to reading historical texts, but getting information from excavated objects was a new experience. It offered insights into people's intimate lives—their pottery, jewellery, tools, statuary, etc. Yes, that's all there. But at the same time, the imprint of the three explanatory strands became popular and remain so to this day among some Indians, although scholars have challenged them.

NAMIT: So can we say that colonial history has a very mixed legacy?

ROMILA: It is very much a mixed legacy. I am making a distinction between (a) exploring and discovering new sources of information on which colonial scholarship did an excellent job, and (b) how they then understood this data, manifest in their explanations of the past, namely how and why events happened. That's what history is based on.

So, on the one hand, one acknowledges the importance of philology, decipherments, epigraphy, archaeology and the new ways of investigating the past that colonial scholarship introduced. On the other hand, the explanatory theories advanced by influential colonial scholars produced a version of history that later scholars found untenable, prompting them to question and revise those interpretations.

NAMIT: Colonial scholars also traced linguistic connections, opening up an entire web of relationships between different populations. Over time, this played a crucial role in shaping how we understand ourselves, didn't it?

ROMILA: Yes, though I find it curious that nobody saw those connections earlier. When Alexander came to north-west India and the kingdoms established in this area had people speaking and writing Greek, as well as others using Sanskrit, it does seem a little surprising that similarities between Greek and Sanskrit languages were not noticed. Even in recent centuries, when William Jones raised the possibility of some links between the two languages, Indian scholars did not comment on the consequences of what was being argued.

NAMIT: That's interesting indeed. Especially if we recall that by Alexander's time, Brahmins knew many languages, including those of the Dravidian group, which were much less connected to Sanskrit than was Greek, spoken by the *mlechbha* (a derogatory term for foreigners and others outside the Vedic social order). Yet, the Brahmins, famed for their understanding of language and grammar, failed to notice such distinctions. Later, they also failed to notice the proximities between Sanskrit and Persian. This suggests that the basic ethos and purpose of their knowledge production was different; it wasn't designed to identify and reflect on such connections, their causes and so on.

ROMILA: Here we encounter another universal feature of societies: the way accounts of the past are pressed into service for particular purposes. Today, historical explanations serve multiple ends. In earlier times, narratives of the past often functioned to record traditions that legitimized those who authored them. That's what the Brahmins also did in their representations of the past, embedding and reinforcing upper-caste perspectives on origins and order. Such legitimizing narratives are woven deeply into early Indian texts.

NAMIT: Right. So the legacy of early historical writing on India is very mixed. It introduced new sources of knowledge and new methods of investigation, but also many unsupported interpretations led by colonial prejudice. Sadly, many of those interpretations are still with us, most notably with the Hindutva view of the past, to which I'll return later.

A female shaman performing exorcisms by Hema Baiga (2023). Baiga tribe in central India.Courtesy: The Crites Collection

2

What Is the Historical Method?

NAMIT: Modernity introduced a new way of thinking about the past. But what gives this approach its power and authority? Why do we see it as more trustworthy than earlier ways? Scholars would argue that it's because of the use of the historical method—a systematic set of practices for establishing facts and interpreting them in context. This method is what distinguishes modern history from older forms of storytelling, as you pointed out earlier. But what exactly is the historical method, and how does it work?

ROMILA: Well, what is the historical method? I think in the early years at Jawaharlal Nehru University (JNU), we were among the first universities that actually had an entire course on the historical method. My students would joke with me because in the first lecture that I would give at the start of the academic year, the freshly recruited students would ask, what should we read? And I would say, go read Agatha Christie's *Death on the Nile* (laughs). And they would look at me with absolute horror and say, what has that got to do with ancient Indian history? And I would say, you read the book and come back, and we will discuss the historical method and then you'll know what the connection is.

NAMIT: So pursuing the historical method is like being a good detective?

ROMILA: Exactly! And more of course. We would then tell our students that as part of the historical method you begin by asking a question or questions about the beginnings, the origins, how something got going or anything else that interests you in the subject you want to know about. Your next step is to ask, what are the sources that are going to tell me about this? And this is where, over the decades, there has been a huge change. When William Jones was writing about those who called themselves Aryas (Aryans), he was only using Vedic sources that were textual and literary. The term 'Aryas' was also used in the Iranian inscriptions of the Achaemenid King Darius in the mid-first millennium BCE.

New sources for exploring the past then emerged through archaeology. In the twentieth century, the Harappan civilization was discovered, which went much further back than the Vedas. One had to figure out who the Harappans were, and were they related at all to the authors of the Vedic texts? This meant an exercise in chronology and ascertaining the kind of society associated with a particular period. Archaeology became increasingly complex—and at the same time, increasingly revelatory. Carbon dating was prevalent by the 1940s as were new techniques, methods, ways of excavation, the reading of data, etc.

When I first started teaching at Delhi University in the 1960s, I remember going to one of the archaeologists of the Archaeological Survey of India, B.K. Thapar, and saying, B.K., I do not understand these archaeological reports of excavations. They are too technical. What do I do? And he said, there is only one thing to do, come and excavate with us. Once you have understood the techniques of excavation and how to read the resulting evidence, you will understand the reports much better. This was, in effect, an invitation to join an excavating team of the ASI, and that is what I did. I taught myself archaeology over a period of three years by joining three seasons of excavations at the Harappan site of Kalibangan in Rajasthan.

So there were new sources. Then by the 1950s, scholars realized that the language used was no longer limited only to Vedic Sanskrit/Old Indo-Aryan. There was Old Iranian-Aryan in north-eastern Iran, which was a cognate of Indo-Aryan. So how were the speakers of Indo-Aryan related to those that spoke this early Iranian-Aryan? Added to this was the introduction of the discipline of linguistics into the study of Vedic Sanskrit. This meant new ways of analysing its words and grammatical structures, and discovering in that process, that not only were there links between some early languages but, more importantly, there were elements of other language systems in Vedic Sanskrit. Dravidian was suggested. And if language X has elements of language Y, the linguistic structure of both languages needs examining, along with new questions about migrations and the mixing of people.

Hydrology and the study of changing river courses, as with the Sutlej, helped to ascertain a region's ecological history. This could provide some evidence of desiccation being one of the factors in the decline of its urban centres. Later, the emergence of genetic science added a new line of evidence. Experts started doing DNA analyses of human remains recovered from graves. Other experts started doing chemical analyses of organic residues to identify details of people's diets and agricultural practices.

NAMIT: Yes, lipid residue analysis is how we know that the Harappans ate beef, pork and laddoos![1] And new technologies continue to expand our sources of evidence. Archaeomagnetic dating, for instance, uses known variations in Earth's magnetic field to determine when an object—such as a hearth—was last heated, offering vital clues about the decline or abandonment of settlements. LiDAR (Light Detection and Ranging) remote sensing technology, mounted on drones, detects subtle shifts in terrain, revealing buried archaeological features like an X-ray scan. Genetic analysis of people from burial sites are illuminating their hierarchies of class and gender, often overturning modern assumptions projected onto prehistoric societies. Zooarchaeology is using animal bones from ancient sites to explore various facets of human-animal relationships. Truly fascinating stuff!

ROMILA: Indeed. So the point I am making is that one of the things we have to tell our students is that one cannot stop with just one source of evidence. Researching a subject means exploring and understanding many kinds of sources that may exist, and the range of evidence they provide and their interrelationships. This is extremely important. This is where the detective mode is most essential. It's important to cross-examine these different sources. Do they all agree with each other? If they differ, then why? What inner contradictions exist? With textual sources, it is important to ascertain whether they are based on eyewitness or second-hand accounts, and what is the vantage point of the author in each case. What are the interests of the author, his audience, his purpose, his reliability and so on. Such cross-examination of multiple sources and clues is central to the historical method. This makes researching history much tougher, but it also opens up a wider horizon than before, when viewing a theme.

Inscriptions add a different complexion to religious and literary texts. Many of them are more reliable as a source for historians than some texts. Why? Because inscriptions remain written in the way they were written 2000 years ago. It is rare that anyone has tampered with them and if so then the tampering will show since inscriptions are largely engraved on stone or on metal. They cannot be changed easily. They largely remain the same. Very often they are dated, which is important. And they generally say straightforward things like so-and-so was ruling and he was ruling well, and he conquered a neighbour in year X, and donated land to so-and-so in year Y, etc. These details are most important. Inscriptions are generally issued as and when a dynasty is stabilized. The inscriptions issued by each ruler of a dynasty, when placed in a chronological order, can provide us with a kind of rough outline or a history of the dynasty.

When examining archaeology, there is the question of the purpose and function of various artefacts, such as grave goods. What do they tell us about the beliefs and the technologies of a society? Does the distribution of objects across graves suggest a social hierarchy? In this detective mode, we rarely know where the inquiry will lead, but each discovery opens up new possibilities. One is, after all, working with entirely new bodies of evidence.

So when teaching the historical method, one has to teach students how to handle these sources. This is the difficult aspect of studying history. It is very difficult to explain all this to somebody who is not fully aware of the significant differences in the sources of history and the caution with which they are to be read. And we even have problems with some modern historians who know one kind of source and cannot understand why we get excited about finding an ancient grave.

Then, after all of this, one has to test the evidence from the sources. Can all this evidence be proved? Is the evidence reliable, as one cannot use unreliable evidence? The properly trained historian can demonstrate that the evidence is reliable.

NAMIT: In other words, are the sources authentic?

ROMILA: Yes. The analysis of evidence is a serious concern for historians. The reliability of evidence based on sources has to be constantly checked. Evidence cannot be based on a myth or hearsay. Historians find myths to be useful not for their recounting of actual events but for the way they often reveal the underlying beliefs and assumptions of a society.

Another important question is: whose history are we researching? As in, which section of society? Written sources tend to come from the educated elites. Historians have often forgotten this and assumed that the entire society observed the way of life described in written texts, whereas many of these texts are limited and represent only one section of society, usually the elite. So the social context of the evidence plays an important role in understanding the text, and in identifying those texts that can be taken as more reliable than others. And while oral information tends to represent a wider cross-section of a society, ascertaining its reliability is more difficult. New methods are being developed today to separate the more reliable oral data from hearsay.

Additionally, languages and scripts evolve over time. Religious and other texts copied or rewritten in newer forms—on perishable material such as birch bark or palm leaves—are susceptible to being changed here and there. Monks in monasteries often did such copying. This requires specialized study by modern scholars. It is not enough to possess only a working knowledge of a classical language. One must also understand its applications and variant forms, as well as the common tropes and rhetorical conventions employed across different genres of texts.

Then, after such analyses comes a stage where one says, right, I have got my sources. I have proved that these sources are authentic. This is what the available clues are telling me. One then starts making causal connections. One must be able to say, this is the evidence for what is being stated as having happened in the past. So, logic and rationality are fundamental to the causal connections one makes from the sources. It's fine to try out various hypotheses but with the strict understanding that they must be discarded if the evidence is shown to be either insufficient or inauthentic. I mean, we all have pet theories about the past and are hesitant to give them up. We often think that our explanations are foolproof, which they generally are not. A critical analysis of explanations is essential to all advances in knowledge and is now used in history as much as in other subjects. This reflects partly the influence of scientific thinking, but just as much the application of plain common sense to data. The logic of everyday life can teach one a lot, though it's also good to remember that common sense is not actually all that common!

Eventually, after you've proved that your sources are both sufficient and genuine, and you've made the causal connections based on them, you then move on to making a historical statement.

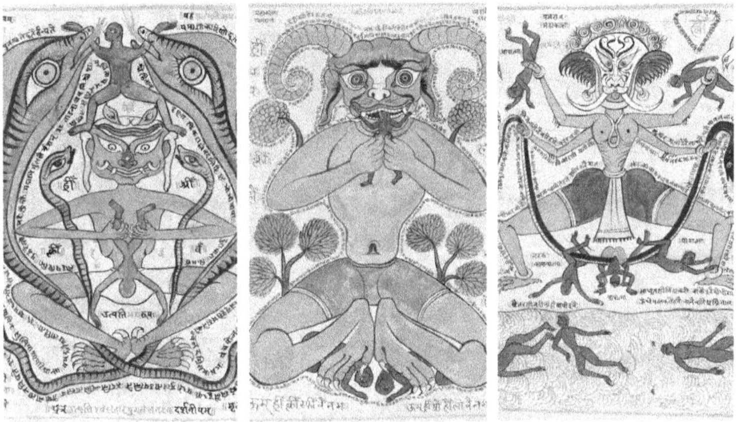

Tantric paintings in a series called 'Cycle of Life' by Kalu Ram (1970s). They show destructive gods punishing and devouring humans in our current dark age of Kali Yuga. Source: QAGOMA, Australia.

3

The Historical Method in Action

NAMIT: To make the historical method even clearer, can you perhaps illustrate it with an example from our world today? Let's consider this hypothetical scenario: a man comes to you and claims that he has read certain court chronicles of Muslim rulers, which include lurid details about their military exploits and religiously motivated violence involving the slaughter of tens of thousands of kafirs. From that, he has concluded that Hindus were systematically targeted and victimized by tyrannical Muslim rulers. How would you use the historical method to assess the legitimacy of his claim?

ROMILA: Well, this is exactly what is being worked on by historians at the moment because this claim of persistent victimization of Hindus by Muslims is widely made in the Hindutva interpretation of medieval history. Is it historically accurate? Have we got the evidence to support the statement? Well, based on the evidence we have, it is not possible to make the claim.

First of all, take the sources most often consulted, that is, the court chronicles of the sultanates of the second millennium CE that are in Persian and some texts that are in Sanskrit, and later in the Indian languages that evolve in these centuries. One has to begin by asking the question: What is the purpose of a chronicle with reference to any court or dynasty? That purpose usually is to praise the ruler, the raja or the sultan and his activities. This is also found in a category of earlier inscriptions called *prashasti*s ('in praise of'), which are laudatory. However unimpressive the ruler's record or activities, they have to make him look good. So, in some cases, the chronicler fantasizes and twists what actually happened in order to satisfy the expectations of the audience of the chronicle. Testing the validity of the chronicle is crucial. It demands that the historian or whoever is quoting from the text must know the language of the text very well and not just casually because the nuance of a particular word has to be considered. One cannot just refer to a killing because it has to be explained through discussing the term that is used, the kind of killing, and its context.

If widespread victimization had indeed taken place, one would expect some details about its forms, as the Persian chroniclers would've waxed eloquent on those descriptions. Yet this is largely missing from the sources. What is also very curious is that if large-scale killings had indeed occurred, one would expect Sanskrit sources to mention the slaughter and its aftermath, and to possibly record intensive complaints. This too is not mentioned. Nothing of the sort is mentioned. What we have instead—in courtly epics such as *Prithviraja Vijaya* or bardic texts such as *Prithviraja Raso*—are occasional references to the Turks as mlecchas, who are described at times as cow-killers or persecutors of Brahmins. But even here, it is seldom clear whether such depictions were meant literally. These phrases often functioned as metaphors or as part of conventional rhetoric—after all, to underscore an enemy's wickedness, one might simply brand him a killer of cows. Also noteworthy is that other sources refer to amicable relations between Hindus and Muslims as craftsmen, as traders, as mercenaries in the armies of both sides, as local and high-level administrators, and to the cementing of relations at elite levels, such as Rajput royal families giving their daughters in marriage to the sultans and the Mughal rulers. Relationships between communities are not singular, simple or universal. They are complex and vary across social levels based on occupation, caste, rituals, trade and various other factors. They often also change over time.

Now, certain Persian chronicles of the early second millennium—and here I'm thinking of accounts by professional writers of eulogies, such as Al-Utbi, Farrukhi Sistani and Gardizi in the court of Mahmud of Ghazni. They mention campaigns in which the sultan is claimed to have killed 50,000 kafirs and/or 50,000 Shias because he is Sunni. In battles of those times, the size of the armies would be smaller, so where does the number 50,000 come from?

NAMIT: Could the number have been large because it included civilian casualties?

ROMILA: No, the reference is to killings on the battlefield. It is a formulaic number because it is frequently repeated, seemingly deployed to indicate a 'successful campaign'. Even with civilian casualties, 50,000 dead would be a serious problem of body disposal. Interestingly, this number is not mentioned in Indian language sources of the time. One assumes that victimization on such scale would have been recorded in non-Persian sources and made much of by the victims. But on the contrary, some donatory inscriptions in the vicinity of Delhi praise the sultans—which indeed may be exaggerated but certainly does not suggest that the sultans were victimizing the population systematically. Occasionally, as I noted earlier, there is a formulaic mention of killing cows or persecuting Brahmins.

So, where do these large figures come from? Can they be taken seriously? Second, if they are victimizing soldiers and armies on the battlefield, or perhaps civilians later on, isn't it strange that the armies of the sultans and the Mughals have significant contingents of Hindu mercenaries and sometimes Rajput commanders? Why would Hindus join an army that was going out to intentionally victimize Hindus for being Hindus?

The point I'm making is that we often don't have simple, straightforward questions or answers. Complex scenarios like these very often point to, if not the answer, the direction in which one has to investigate a problem.

NAMIT: That's very insightful. Let me summarize this in my own terms. Let's say we are asked to investigate an alleged claim in a medieval Turko–Persian court chronicle about a sultan indulging in a large-scale killing of Hindu kafirs. We would begin, as we must always do, by reflecting on the nature of our sources, their typical purpose, the stylistic devices used in them and so on. Take court chronicles, for example. Their purpose is often to glorify the military, sexual and religious exploits of monarchs. The size of the army is frequently inflated. Grandiose titles and praises are heaped upon the king. Hyperbole and ceremony are often baked into such writing. Likewise, for the *prashasti*s, which often glorify the rulers. So this aspect of the source is important to consider. But the claim in the court chronicle could still be entirely true, so we continue our investigation.

We then have to understand the context of the killings claimed, whether of soldiers or unarmed civilians. Linguistic expertise in the semantics of older and regional registers of Persian would be necessary. What kinds of weapons and firearms (if any) were used? Our scepticism would increase if casualties are claimed in a formulaic way, or if the victim's side mentions no victimization, or if the composition of the armies and their commanders don't suggest a conflict mostly based on religion. Even the notorious invader Mahmud of Ghazni (971–1030) employed Hindu mercenaries who lived in a Hindu quarter in Ghazna. One of Mahmud's regiments, much feared in Central Asia, was commanded by a Hindu warrior named Tilak.

And it's often the case that even when religious rhetoric is deployed—whether as slogans in the heat of war, or later by court chroniclers—upon investigating further, one finds evidence for other answers. For instance, that the primary factors driving an offensive war or raid were often the old-fashioned imperatives of increasing territorial control, tax revenue or acquiring booty—not so much religious zeal or animosity, which may be present but not as a primary factor.

So the full spectrum of detective work needs to be done in dispassionately assessing the truth of a claim. If various clues don't add up during our detective work, if too many gaps and contradictions appear, it casts doubt on the claims of the court chronicle itself. Conversely, if the clues add up, those claims will get fortified.

Finally, if our investigation substantiates the court chronicle's claim with high confidence—showing that the ruler did commit sectarian violence against civilians—one should neither whitewash the act nor divorce it from its historical context. To this end, we must ask: How does it compare with other instances of royal violence in the medieval era, whether by the Cholas, Vijayanagar kings, the Marathas or others? How frequent were such acts under this ruler? Were they concentrated in his initial, expansionary phase of conquest or did they recur throughout his reign? Such questions help scholars assess and position specific acts of violence within the larger historical narrative of the period.

ROMILA: Yes. Let's consider another example: the Battle at Haldighati (1576). It is always projected by certain groups of people as being in essence, a Hindu–Muslim conflict, in which the brave Hindus defended the glory of India.

Any historian who tries to understand this conflict must sift through all available primary and secondary sources. They have to be mindful of how their medieval authors' interests might have coloured a source—to uncover deeper layers: what triggered the conflict, which groups joined either side, what were their motivations, how did the battle unfold, what were its broader consequences and so on. On examining the context, for instance, one finds that the Mughal army was led by two Rajputs. Rana Pratap's army had a contingent led by descendants of the Suri rulers, who were Muslims—their general, Hakim Khan Suri, died in that battle.

How can we treat this as just a Hindu–Muslim conflict? It was a complex political conflict in which all kinds of political entities were involved on each side. If we are to know more about the war and what instigated it, we cannot reduce it to a mere Hindu–Muslim conflict. We have to look at the intricacies of the political relationships that were also governing the conflict.

NAMIT: Indeed. Another example is the Battle of Talikota (1565), in which four Deccan sultanates—Bijapur, Bidar, Ahmadnagar and Golconda—defeated Vijayanagar. That wasn't a simple Hindu–Muslim conflict either, though some people doggedly see it that way. The armies of the sultanates had Hindus, such as the Marathas of Bijapur and Telugus of Golconda. Vijayanagar's armies had many Muslim and Christian mercenaries. The warring sultans and rajas in this battle had previously been allies, acting against other sultans and rajahs in an ever-shifting political chessboard. Incidentally, the framing of this battle as a Hindu–Muslim conflict also came from a colonial historian, Robert Sewell (1845–1925), in his book *A Forgotten Empire (Vijayanagar): A contribution to the History of India.* His work was very much in the lineage of James Mill. And the communal cast he gave to this battle was lapped up by Hindu nationalists because it served their politics and prejudices.

Can you perhaps also talk about Mahmud of Ghazni, who many Indians see as a fanatic warrior, a destroyer of temples and plunderer of their wealth? This view of him comes from Turko–Persian chronicles. His desecration of the Somanatha Temple in 1026 CE is, in fact, central to Hindu nationalists' animus against Muslims, and to claims of the Hindu community's lingering 'social trauma' and 'memories of humiliation'. But doesn't this have a complex backstory—plus a deft manufacturing of social memory—where colonial writers have played a major role? How has the historical method illuminated this episode?

ROMILA: Persian court chronicles and certain other Persian texts say that Mahmud of Ghazni raided the temple of Somanatha and several others, looting and destroying them. But, notably, the narrative of the raid differs substantially from one text to another. There is little agreement on what actually happened.

The British discovered these accounts in the nineteenth century and created a narrative about the raids. They did not consult the sources in Sanskrit, although there are many that are relevant. Consider the Jain minister of the Solanki king of Gujarat persuading the king to rebuild the Somanatha Temple. What is fascinating, however, are the reasons given for the poor condition of the original temple—that it was no longer properly maintained, and located as it was on the shore, it had suffered from weathering by the sea spray. Mahmud is not mentioned, although this account was written only a couple of centuries after.

Or take a source quite close to Mahmud's raid. This is the account of a pilgrimage to the temple by the Kadamba king ruling in the region of Goa, just twelve years after the raid. It does not mention Mahmud's raid, nor any damage to the temple.

Other sources include many Sanskrit inscriptions found in the vicinity. Some of these mention the Bohras, the Arab–Gujarati trading community descended from merchants who had long settled there. A lengthy bilingual inscription was issued by a Persian ship's captain, Nuruddin Feroz, requesting some land for building a mosque for those settled in the area. The local council, consisting of Hindu dignitaries and administrators, agreed to do so. Some of the land so granted is linked to the Somanatha Temple estates. What is clear from these inscriptions is that the civil authority was Hindu and was in complete control of the area and that Somanatha was a flourishing commercial centre. None of the Hindu or Jain texts mention a raid on Somanatha by Mahmud, which is odd, to say the least.

In quoting these sources my intention is not to deny Mahmud's raid on Somanatha just because it is not mentioned in important Sanskrit sources but to question the historical narrative that was later constructed and the meaning that was given to it in modern times.

Around five centuries after the raid, a body of stories emerged, drawn largely from the oral traditions of western Uttar Pradesh. Many of these revolve around a figure called Ghazi Miyan, portrayed as a nephew of Mahmud of Ghazni—an entirely fictitious claim, since Mahmud had no such nephew. In these tales, Ghazi Miyan is depicted as a benefactor to the local population. Here is an example of the recording of a folk tale with no historical basis. Fortunately, historian Shahid Amin has worked on it in *Conquest and Community: The Afterlife of Warrior Saint Ghazi Miyan*. He did not dismiss it, nor did he refer to it as a historical event. He investigated why such a story was imagined and circulated. This is the significant question that historians have to ask if the event remains unproven.

In the nineteenth century, a colonial version of this 'history' was also constructed. Mill's two-nation theory became axiomatic, shaping British perceptions and even colouring the debate in the House of Commons in 1843, where the raid on Somanatha was first discussed. The colonial version that emerged was one-sided, based only on Persian texts, and it cast the episode as part of an imagined, perpetual Hindu–Muslim conflict deemed foundational to Indian history. The account went largely unchallenged; even nationalist writers later absorbed it, as seen in K.M. Munshi's *Somanatha: The Shrine Eternal* (1965). Decades later, some even sought to legitimize the demolition of the Babri Masjid by presenting it as symbolic vengeance for Mahmud's raid.[2]

Challenging the colonial version meant considering sources that had been ignored, including Sanskrit inscriptions and Hindu and Jain texts. This opened up new questions: How did

the temple, despite Mahmud's raid, emerge as a major trading centre where the local Hindu ruler and other Gujaratis actively traded with Persian and Arab merchants? What had priority for Mahmud—looting the temple's wealth, or destroying or taking away its idols? Or some combination of both?
And how do the answers here change the historical narrative?

NAMIT: This episode is so interesting. I mean, if this raid on Somanatha was truly as traumatic for Hindus as colonial writers and Hindu nationalists later claimed, why was it not even recorded by Hindus at the time? If such records had ever existed and were later lost, we would still expect to find some references of them in other surviving texts—but these haven't come to light. Whatever the reality of the raid, what seems clear is that Hindu texts did not preserve its memory. It was only when the British unearthed accounts of Mahmud's campaigns in Turko–Persian chronicles and discussed them in Parliament that Hindu revivalists seized on this narrative and gave it new life. Until then, Hindus appear to have carried no memory of these temple raids—at least nothing resembling the accounts in Turko–Persian chronicles, nor any sense of collective 'trauma' or 'humiliation.'

How does one explain the omission of Mahmud's raid on Somanatha in Indian chronicles of the time, or the amnesia of Brahmanical elites (other Indians would have cared far less about it)? An obvious possibility is that the raid was not all that traumatic, nor was the damage to the temple all that great. The locals simply rebuilt and carried on business as usual—much as their ancestors had done when rival kings within the subcontinent had raided and pillaged their wealthy temples as spoils of war. The Persian court chronicles could well be embellished accounts. That may be why the Goan Hindu king, visiting the Somanatha Temple twelve years after the raid, saw nothing unusual enough to merit a comment. Or perhaps the local Gujaratis of the day saw trading as far more lucrative than nurturing bad memories and grievances.

The British clearly had a vested interest in playing up these raids. They cited them to present their colonial project as more 'enlightened' and to divide and rule Indians. It suited their theory of two nations in perpetual conflict, as you noted. Hindu revivalists then forged the trope of the 'thousand years of memory' and its lingering 'social trauma'. This fictional 'wound' to the 'Hindu psyche' was inflamed further when former deputy prime minister of India, L.K. Advani, launched his Ram Rath Yatra from Somanatha. A textbook example of how memories and emotions can be manufactured—and weaponized—for political ends.

ROMILA: It is in grappling with such complex questions that the historical method becomes absolutely indispensable. Let me just sum up its main steps briefly. The first is to choose a subject worth researching and identifying aspects of it that can be questioned and analysed. The second is to collect the relevant sources and verifying their authenticity. The third is to interrogate the sources, extracting the answers, and organizing them in a way that reveals the rational and logical patterns they contain. Finally, to formulate a historical statement from this body of evidence.

NAMIT: Thank you for illustrating the historical method with some examples. To me, it's really another name for a logical–rational way that makes investigations of the past more rigorous and reliable—and always open to revision if new evidence or better interpretations turn up. I really like your metaphor of detective work!

Madhubani painting. Credit: Chiring Chandan, CC BY-SA 4.0

4

What Constitutes Trustworthy History?

NAMIT: Many readers also face another challenge. History is not like the physical sciences and cannot be as 'objective'. I mean, a theory in physics or chemistry can be overturned, but the new theory is then expected to be universally valid and verifiable.

History, however, is a social science and has different epistemological foundations. It comes with its own distinctive subjectivity. We saw this with colonial scholarship. Marxist interpretations, too, variously blend the objective and the subjective. And that's partly because historical accounts are influenced by the historian's ethical and social values, which are partly shaped by the prevailing zeitgeist. Historians might prefer a less or a more charitable interpretation of an event, depending on their sympathies. Their narratives are also shaped by their social location and the dynamics of power and knowledge that make up some of their social context. So, even with the same facts, historians often bring different perspectives in assessing causes and effects and reach different understandings of the past.

Partly due to such different subjective vantage points and emphases, the discipline of history has produced many schools of historiography worldwide. In India, for example, we have the colonial, nationalist, Marxist, subaltern, postcolonial, and more recently, feminist, Ambedkarite, environmental and other schools. Even when working with the same set of sources whose veracity no one doubts, scholars across these historiographies often differ in their reading of them and employ different mixes of cultural and material factors to explain past events and beliefs. Their narratives possess varying explanatory power, which often complement each other but not always. Sometimes they simply disagree.

The general reader often feels overwhelmed by all this. How should one navigate the subjectivity and diverse explanations across these different schools of historiography? To many, it makes history seem too malleable and manipulable. In short, how can a general reader reliably identify trustworthy history?

ROMILA: It is a tough question. I remember giving talks at the Indian Institute of Science in Bangalore, and at the request of the students, I also gave a short course on history and spoke about the historical method. In the very first session, a hand went up in the audience, and the student said, we all know about the scientific method, but there is no such thing as a historical method. I said, but I am talking to you about the historical method. And he said, no, I see one basic difference. In science, if an experiment doesn't work, it collapses, it's thrown out. What happens in history is that you chaps carry on with it. I said, no, we don't! That's the point about modern interpretations of history.

The reason why we do not teach from books that were published a hundred years ago is because their understanding of the problem, the historical problem, was either incomplete or faulty or from a point of view in which the sources were limited in those days. I mean, for example, who today reads only Max Müller on the Aryan question? If they do so, they are deliberately cutting themselves off from recent research, which has altered our approach to the sources of the question. And yet, as we know, there is a big debate going on where many who follow the Hindutva ideology keep insisting that the Aryans originated in India and were not migrants from Central Asia.

Now, what is the solution to this? We can't demonstrate history in a lab. But the basic thing about the scientific method is that even when an experiment fails, you have to explain the reason for the failure. You can't just say, oh, I did this experiment, it failed and so I'm getting rid of it. You have to go into the details of why it failed or, if it succeeded, why it succeeded. In the same way, in the historical method, you put out a hypothesis, you go through the steps that I indicated, and you come up with a generalization and say, therefore, this happened or did not happen.

Someone else comes along and says that various sources were not consulted. Therefore, the reading should be different and immediately there is a debate. Now, the general reader has to be told that history is not the story of interpretations that cannot be doubted or questioned. That in every generation of historians, questions are asked about what the earlier generation may have said. Asking questions should not take the form of blaming and abusing others. You have to debate the issue, and you have to say, this is why I think your reading is faulty, or this is why I accept it.

Unless you do that, you are not only deceiving yourself but also the reader. If the reader knows that there is an ongoing debate on the subject, and X has said this and Y has said that, then they are aware of the fact that there are conflicting opinions which the reader has to be familiar with before deciding to accept or reject the historical statement. The reader has to be aware of the conflict, be able to evaluate the authenticity of the sources quoted, know why there is a conflict, what the conflict suggests, what it might lead to, etc., etc. The attempt is to understand the reason for the conflict. It is a different approach to knowledge from what it was a couple of centuries ago. Fundamentally, what we have to understand is that a historical narrative is a piece of knowledge that is there to be further questioned. It's not about being nasty to X or Y because of disagreement with them for unspecified reasons.

All knowledge has to be questioned. This is something we haven't quite understood in this country. We cannot block off any knowledge and say, this is not to be questioned. All knowledge has to be questioned. Once you get to that point, then whenever you pick up a book and start reading it, at the back of your mind you are thinking of questions, and that's the best way of reading the book.

NAMIT: That's a great point. All knowledge has to be questioned—especially when it makes claims about truth and reality that may have adverse consequences for others.

Alright, so our sources and historical knowledge have been expanding. The questions we ask change over time, as do many earlier interpretations. But for the lay reader, this isn't always a case of the explanations becoming 'truer' or 'more reliable', is it? This happens, say, when the interpretations come from two very different ethical value systems coexisting in the same generation, like famously in economics with the Harvard–MIT School versus the Chicago School, and their distinctly different approaches at one time to explaining economic outcomes of the past, the role of the market, state spending and taxation, and so on.

Similarly, if you have, say, highly conservative historians who have little problem with patriarchy. They may well believe, rightly or wrongly, that while certain extremes—such as sati, or preventing menstruating women from entering temples—are unacceptable, traditional patriarchy is still a positive thing for giving stability to family and society. Or they might believe similar things about the hierarchy of caste, that while untouchability is bad, much of the rest is worthwhile. They might argue that it saves people from the ravages of economic competition, that identities of caste create a much-needed sense of belonging. Or take a historian like Niall Ferguson and his apologia for British colonialism.

I mean, it is often said that historians should avoid making value judgments. Yet historians are human, and their moral frameworks inevitably shape how they understand the past and formulate interpretations—interpretations they naturally regard as rational. For the lay reader, this can make it difficult to reconcile the often-divergent views of different historians.

ROMILA: Why should the reader want to reconcile them?

NAMIT: Should the reader just let them be?

ROMILA: Let them be, provided they are debated as historical concepts and not as slogans of social and religious ideologues.

NAMIT: So, the reader should be able to look at both, or many, such accounts and decide which is better. That puts the burden of identifying smart history on the reader's knowledge and intellectual sophistication. That's not easily scalable, is it?

ROMILA: (nods) I mean, even if you look at something like science, there are some issues, notable issues on which there are differing points of view and opinions, and the attitude is, well, they are there for people to assess their validity. Each is examined in turn, and the degree of its conviction is considered. So, if there are four different ways of interpreting something, as in the Rashomon effect in that classic Japanese film, each story has to be told, and people then judge its validity. And the judgement is not arbitrary. I mean, we don't just pick someone from the street and ask for their opinion. Some basic knowledge is required which then provides the involvement with the question being discussed.

There are knowledgeable people who argue over a subject. What we must get over is the question—and I am often asked this—how can you have different interpretations in history if the facts are the same? But interpretations may differ because they depend on how those facts are read, analysed, and explained.

Interpretations are not simply a matter of personal preference; they emerge from careful reasoning, shaped by the methods we use to examine evidence. What matters is that these interpretations are laid out for the reader in a rational, logical way, with the methodology made clear. That is important.

NAMIT: Yes, I think that's the crucial point. Even when a historical interpretation has subjective aspects—which is inevitable—it still needs to be supported by the best evidence and the most rational arguments that the historian can muster.

You know, I love that analogy you made with the Rashomon story. Are you willing to go on record for saying that history has a Rashomon-like quality to it?

ROMILA: Yes (smiles). I still have the right to maintain that a particular interpretation of the facts is more convincing than others—so long as I can demonstrate the reliability of my sources and the validity of the causal connections I draw.

NAMIT: What I hear you saying is that the ambiguities of life, our partial knowledge of events and our particular vantage points lend all narratives about the past something of a Rashomon-like quality but with a key distinction: Not all narratives can be called legitimate histories. A credible *historical* interpretation must adhere to the standards of the historical method and be based on a rational reading of all available evidence. Only then do such diverse but well-founded interpretations, taken together, offer a richer and more pluralistic understanding of the historical event—even as 'the truth' might remain elusive. I resonate with this view!

Temple of Ghatiya Dai ji with devotees, ber (jejube) tree, ghosts and spirits, a black leopard by Ramrati Bai Baiga (2021), Baiga tribe of eastern Madhya Pradesh. Courtesy: The Crites Collection.

5

Marxist Historiography and the Class/Caste Debate

NAMIT: Prof. Thapar, many people call you a 'Marxist historian'. As you know, right-wing folks have turned this into a term of abuse, even though Marxist historiography is a powerful framework for understanding the past through its material realities, economic structures and social class relations. They often also ignorantly conflate a scholar's reliance on Marxist historiography with being a political Marxist. How much affinity do you feel for this school of historiography and has that affinity changed over time?

ROMILA: That is a very tough question to answer. Because you know, you may identify with one school that seems adequate, but then you encounter new sources that raise fresh questions and force you to see things differently. Do you acknowledge the shift, or do you cling to the old view and ignore the new data? In my experience of reading and thinking for fifty or sixty years, no interpretation can claim to be right for all time across all subjects. Every interpretation is shaped by the kind of analysis one undertakes. At times, a reading from one perspective may appear almost perfect—until another perspective proves just a little sharper. Sometimes the difference is merely one of nuance or emphasis; at other times, it can be quite substantial.

So one has to be a little open about that. And I guess this was brought home to me very strongly in the '60s and '70s, when I attended conferences in the Department of Social Sciences in UNESCO. In those days, they had many conferences on challenging subjects. I met numerous French scholars who identified as Marxists, though they were variously described as structural Marxists, neo-Marxists or some other kind of Marxist. At first, I wondered—does one have to detail the kind of Marxist one may be? I mean, surely it is enough to state that one either is, or is not, a Marxist. This applies not just to Marxism but to any theoretical explanation one may adhere to.

When I began talking to the scholars, I understood better. I recall a particularly engaging conversation about gift exchange, a practice that was economically central to many early societies. Goods circulated not only as commodities but also as gifts, raising the question: what exactly does gift exchange mean in such contexts? One Marxist explanation emphasizes, quite rightly, the social hierarchy it reflects—those of higher status who own and bestow the gift, and those who labour to produce it. How, then, do the former secure the labour that generates the resources embodied in the gift? What rules regulate this relationship? This line of reasoning is straightforward and viable. Yet others argue that control is rooted less in economics than in religious meaning: that authority is sanctioned and enforced through sacred frameworks. So the central question becomes whether the patron's power to command labour rests on economic reasons, religious ideology, or a fusion of both.

At one level, the explanation is clearly economic; yet it also rests on the patron's superior position in the social hierarchy, often reinforced by religious associations linked to economic activity. A strict Marxist might argue that the fundamental tie between patron and labourer lies in the necessity of labour for production. Still, to ignore the additional socio-religious dimensions would be to miss other forces at play—even if they operate in lesser ways. On this very question of gift exchange, I had several stimulating conversations with the historian Ram Sharan Sharma, exploring what might count as a Marxist reading of the various categories of *dāna* (gifts and donations). The examples we examined covered a wide spectrum, revealing how layered and complex the practice could be.

So I think it is difficult to identify precisely which school of historiography a historian belongs to, unless it is specified, or the reasons for belonging to it are stated, because there are many occasions when one prioritizes different kinds of analysis in order to explore a question. But a broad association is always possible.

NAMIT: Is it then fair to say that around the pillar of Marxist analysis, you have had often, even frequently, occasion to expand your analysis to test other explanations, ones belonging to the religio-cultural realm, for instance?

ROMILA: Yes. Or let me bring in another aspect.

For example, when writing early history, the economic relationship between those who labour to produce resources and those who control the finished product—using it to generate wealth through sale or exchange—is far from straightforward. There are variations shaped by other activities, or activities with hidden economic dimensions that have to be teased out. These additional factors complicate the picture, and historians must remain attentive to how they intersect with economic and social relations. The greater the diversity of goods produced and exchanged, the more complex the functioning of society becomes. But such complexity cannot be ignored. It must be investigated, weighed, and assessed—what carries greater, equal, or lesser significance, and how these dynamics alter or influence one another. Much of history lies in understanding this interface across diverse sources.

Economic forms that shape the structure of society are central to understanding how it functions. Even before Marx, archaeology made this amply clear. Cultures are defined by multiple features that must be identified and related to one another—for instance, the resources on which a society depends and who controls them, the gradations of social levels, the hierarchies that emerge and so on. Recognizing this is not economic determinism; it is plain common sense. We see it in every kind of society, and we differentiate societies by examining these forms. This in itself is not Marxist historiography, which emphasizes particular patterns that determine the social and economic structures of societies. Rather, it is the domain of economic and social history. Some historians limit themselves to studying these forms, others extend their scope to include belief systems and rituals that brings in what is initially a different activity, but which often finds a niche in the socio-economic pattern and can become a dominant part of that.

NAMIT: Yeah, I've read some Marxist historians who've looked at the caste system and tended to reduce its distinct religious-metaphysical dimension to its class elements by saying that the ultimate motive behind this system is to more reliably extract cheap labour from the lower classes, etc. In effect, culture as a conjoined but partly independent motive force in shaping human affairs is neglected—and it remains largely a material, class-based explanation. How do you approach this caste vs. class question?

ROMILA: Well, I have had problems with the subject of caste and class because some historians of ancient India disapprove of my saying that caste cannot be equated with class. I maintain that these are categories that partially overlap and are therefore not entirely separate, but they overlap here and there and in different ways. The origins of each are different. When analysing a situation in the Indian past, one can't analyse it solely in class terms; one has to look at the presence of caste. And when one is analysing caste, one can't look at it only as caste; one has to consider in juxtaposition the implications of a possible class analysis. One has to look at what contributes to a class status and how this relates to the social context. Therefore, one can't invariably equate caste and class. The two are in some ways, and up to a point, intertwined, and this must be explained.

NAMIT: Do you mind explaining that, as in how you see the origins of caste, its evolution and how you've approached it as something that is distinct from class?

ROMILA: Okay, let me try and explain the point I am attempting to make at greater length and go back to how we have studied caste. I shall try and simplify my argument.

The term 'caste' refers to an important basis on which Indian society has been organized. Every society has a structure and rules according to which the different parts of the structure function. Caste-based society in India combines two distinct but related concepts: *varna* and *jati*. Varna is the hierarchy of the entire society. It is divided into *savarna*, comprising groups that have access to a varna/caste identity and the *avarna*, who lack such an identity. In modern times, avarna refers to Dalits and adivasis, and the segregation is attributed to the savarnas being pure in origin and the avarnas being polluted. This latter category exists very insistently among the constitutionally defined category of Hindus but is also present in Muslim, Christian and Sikh communities. Varna counts four levels, the highest being the Brahmins, then the Kshatriyas, the Vaishyas and the Shudras. These four groups have sometimes been spoken of as being status groups. Varna is technically a status acquired at birth from parentage, but there have been a few instances of a higher status being acquired through performing rituals and certain lifestyle changes.

There is also the reference to the functioning group called *jati*. Jati has its own structure and hierarchy although it can be linked with varna. The status comes specifically from birth, as the term 'jati' implies. It is consulted for the rites of passage—birth, marriage and death rituals. There is segregation between the savarnas and the avaranas, such that the latter were victimized by the former in terms of their being permitted only the lowest occupations and treated as highly polluted and therefore untouchable.

Caste did not begin as a full-fledged, self-created system defined by religion and serving religious purposes. The earliest mention of the four varnas does come from a religious text, a hymn in the Rigveda, the earliest of the Vedas dated to about 1200 BCE. However, most Vedic scholars have argued that this hymn was added to the text at a much later date. What was added therefore was not ideas about how caste began but the pattern as it had been worked out from the four varnas. My question is: what existed prior to the four varnas and how was such an early society organized? We may not know the social formation, but we have a few clues from the later rules.

One characteristic of caste that differentiates it from class is that caste identity, expressed as jati, is based on birth and nothing can change it. Rules of marriage probably grew alongside the observances of endogamy and exogamy, with a turn to patriliny or matriliny. Occupations tended to get slotted into status as in many societies, and differentiation was sometimes legitimized through religious ritual which introduced the slow entry of religious factors into caste. This could have been a simple form of social functioning prior to the classification of varna. This classification may have introduced the need to legitimize the system through resort to religious ritual. I am suggesting that this may have come later because there are texts that specifically refer to social concerns and practices, such as the edicts of Ashoka, which do not refer to either jati or varna. Megasthenes, the Greek ambassador to the Mauryan court around 300 BCE, when describing social divisions does not follow the structure of varna. His description seems to carry a flavour more of jati than of varna. This was possibly still a period when divisions based on the distinctions of jati were recognized, but not as yet given the authoritative stamp of varna. Was this an attempt by a non-Indian to try and figure out a system of social divisions that was eventually to be based firmly on castes?

References to varna in the *Dharmashastras* are well established by the early first millennium CE. The differences of opinion between Brahmanical thinkers and their *nastika* critics, who rejected the authority and sanctity of the Vedas, were recognized. Possibly this was the period when the Brahmanical exposition of varna and its rules were more fully formulated. Simpler forms of social systems are familiar from the Mahabharata and the Ramayana, in the context of early systems of clan societies and incipient kingdoms. Clans, as described in the Mahabharata, are less convoluted than some of the later societies that were more likely early kingdoms. Clans would still have been governed by assemblies of elders of equal status—the *gana-rajya*s and the *gana-sangha*s, and suchlike, whereas the kingdoms registered the rise of particular families who eventually established their power. One could inquire whether the slow takeover of the earlier forms of social organization by more complex forms of kingship required formulating a society functioning with new rules and perhaps at this point the varna scheme came into existence.

In the formulation of varna, the central pivot is the concept of hierarchy, divided into two unequal groups: the savarnas, who had a varna identity, and the avaranas, who were denied one. This division would have given tremendous power to whoever controlled the upper segment and, inevitably, it was the Brahmins who controlled its formulation and the rules. They were the authors of the *Dharmashastras*. The two segments became a sharp division in society, with each having entirely separate functions. The religious legitimation probably made the control of the Brahmins more acceptable, and thereby the upper castes became much stronger through this hierarchy sanctioned by religion.

It is not very clear as to exactly when the underlining of purity and pollution became so central to the division of the varna into two. Logically it would have come when the varna system was established. Was this idea introduced not only to strengthen the distinction between the two groups but more to legitimize the distinction as absolute and irrevocable? Occupations, especially those requiring manual labour, could be relegated to those slotted as impure people, who were not only individually impure but were born into communities that were treated as impure. Impurity was secured by being given a hereditary origin. It is not clear how jati fits into the structure of a varna-based society and especially if it was a subdivision of varna as it is sometimes taken to be. Could they possibly have been parallel systems where jati was the rule in rites of passage and varna in matters of status and rank. The word 'jati' implies identity by birth, which is of course characteristic of clan society, so possibly its origins lay in the clans which may have been the format that the jati as caste followed. Possibly jati was viewed as the smaller, more manageable functional unit, initially unslotted into the varnas and ranked largely through occupations. Each category had its own hierarchy specific to the local, regional distribution of groups. Was the totality of varna in an enormous society difficult to handle for the functions of everyday life and therefore the jati became the unit? Whereas for the larger social totality, the perception and perhaps even the functioning in some instances was based on the *Dharmashastra* rules?

What I am trying to suggest is that we tend to always treat caste as an extension of Hinduism and deeply entwined in religion. Was it so? Should we now try to reverse it and see how it holds if caste is the functional social formation and religion is an extension? This will also require a study of how caste—both the equivalent of jati and of varna—functions in the context of Islam and Christianity in India. These studies need doing in depth.

Can we see caste as initially just a system of organizing society and then see the 'when' and 'why' of the introduction of the religio-ritual aspect to ensure perpetuity? Since there seems not to have been any conversion, how were people recruited to

Hinduism? And if caste is essential, then how is it allotted if identity comes from birth? We have focused on the study of varna but perhaps we should give more attention to jati. Also, let us not forget that social systems are never static. We have assumed caste to be static but was it? Caste has a history, and this in itself would have evolved into changing patterns alongside historical change. The Kshatriya varna seems to have been rather open with many who came to power in various ways claiming this status. Shivaji, the Maratha ruler, is an example, where the status was bestowed on him. The question of mobility needs to be investigated far more as also the question of whether it applied to both varna and jati or only varna. Caste viewed from a historical perspective and the changes it underwent remains to be studied further.

There are also some interesting seeming contradictions in its functioning. The avarna, denied a varna identity, were regarded as low caste, untouchable and impure. This was an indication of their dismal position in the social hierarchy. Yet, there were others, the ascetics and renouncers, who tried to expunge their varna identity. They desired a liberation from caste. Despite their not claiming a varna identity, they were highly respected members of society. The ideal life-time curriculum, especially for the Brahmins and upper castes, was observing the four *ashramas* (stages of life: brahmacharya, grhastha, vanaprastha and sannyasa), where the last one—sannyasa—required the person to forego all identities and take to a wandering life in the wilderness. He was in effect an avarna, although not called that and without the social disabilities associated with the avarna. Living alone in the wilderness appears not to have been the choice of most elderly people, as it is infrequently depicted in the literature, and it probably remained a rather distant ideal not observed by many. Becoming a monk or a nun is not the same thing, as this involved joining another kind of community.

One of the most fascinating aspects of such a study will be to observe the patterns of culture that emerge. We have often spoken about regional differences in the subcontinent and their effect on historical factors. But we have to consider that when there were major historical changes, not just invasions but also others resulting from migrations, changes in the environment, trade routes, mutating economies and multiple religious movements in the form of new sects of preachers, then what affect did these changes have on the men and women who were the people of that region?

NAMIT: That's excellent food for thought on the origins and the interface of jati and varna. Their coming together to form the caste system that's familiar to us indeed involved some melding of a group's occupational labour with notions of ritual purity and pollution. The latter likely became the organizing principle for a new kind of hierarchy among groups—which included clans, tribes or occupational guilds—some of which may well have been weakly endogamous earlier while having no structured hierarchy. Over time, new castes came into existence as new professions arose, or tribes were integrated into caste society.

Now, the presence of various groups is one thing, but it seems that it was through the concept of purity/pollution associated with Brahmanism that—as it caught on—society began to emphasize endogamy, exploding the number of jatis, placing them in a hierarchical relation to each other and on the varna scale. In any case, one can't really reduce caste to class. They interact and overlap in ways that have to be carefully teased out, as you've suggested. More generally, cultural complexity is not reducible to material reality.

Going back to my question of what school of historiography you identify with, I just want to add one thing after your explanation. I know people call you a Marxist historian, but I've recently discovered that at least one prominent Marxist historian thinks it is a factual error to describe you as such! (laughs) You know, I've been reading you for decades and I've long had my own doubts too. So it's good to hear your clarification. I think that over time you've focused not just on political economy but also on culture. You've in fact embraced an increasingly composite approach and have analysed culture on its own terms—as a sphere with its own distinct logic and autonomy in shaping events, rather than one driven solely by material/economic factors.

Gond art depicted on a wall, State Tribal Museum, Bhubaneswar.
Photo: Namit Arora (2022).

6

On the Importance of Interdisciplinary History

NAMIT: Until a century or so ago, most historians saw history as an account of political events, dynasties and religions led by 'great men'. But then things began changing. Other emerging fields such as sociology, anthropology, psychology, economics and ecology began influencing historians, who started factoring in other human realities and data to provide a richer portrait of our past. And so began the rise of interdisciplinary history, which is now an integral part of historical studies worldwide.

Our discussion so far has already implied the importance of interdisciplinary history, but let's zoom into it further. The early pioneers of social and economic history, such as Eric Hobsbawm and E.P. Thompson, investigated class structures, labour conditions and various economic forces to develop their historical explanations, usually employing a Marxist lens. The Annales School, led by scholars such as Marc Bloch and Lucien Febvre, emphasized geography, economics and social conditions as the key drivers of history. I know you have leaned on these and other approaches. Since then, a new set of historical questions have drawn on various disciplines for answers and have changed how historical scholarship is now pursued. How would you describe these changes and the value they provide?

ROMILA: Many new aspects of historical writing have become important in the last half century and they have expanded the approach of professional historians. I think we can speak of two significant changes. The first one we have already talked about, namely, the insistence on using the historical method to critically examine a historical question.

The second change is the turn to using an interdisciplinary approach. Relevant data is no longer limited to historical sources but also includes patterns of analysis and models that come from disciplines with proximities to history, such as archaeology, linguistics, genetics, sociology, economic history, ecology and the history of religion. This is often introduced by including history as one of many disciplines in the social sciences that inform each other.

These two changes are what really separate Indology from the modern understanding of history. Indology refers to the colonial era enterprise that mainly focused on studying Indian texts, languages and religions and tended to privilege scriptures, epics and elite literature. Today's discipline of history goes far beyond the narrow scope of Indology through its range of sources, questions, tools, methods, analysis, interdisciplinary approaches and so on.

The emergence of the social sciences is in itself only about a century old and the disciplines that are relevant to history from its list may increase as new knowledge enters the social sciences.

The interdisciplinary approach in history can use multiple disciplines to gain new sources and patterns of explanation. This approach is used only by a minority of those who are not trained as historians yet write history. It may be used, for instance, in deciphering unknown scripts. The careful person here sets out the procedures borrowed from other disciplines—linguistics in this case—and observes the rules, where relevant, of these disciplines. As a result, it is possible to have a meaningful discussion with such a person. However, if the person is using a hit-or-miss method without any rules, then discussion becomes counterproductive.

NAMIT: Can you perhaps cite some examples, as in specific themes or questions that have benefited from an interdisciplinary approach, where scholars have gone beyond their reliance on merely 'historical sources' to improve their explanations?

ROMILA: Sure. Take, for instance, how we know about economic changes in early society. They are best viewed through stages of archaeological change that may also draw on data from anthropological studies of social change. The earliest societies in the subcontinent that we know of comprise hunter-gatherers in the Narmada region. Their material needs were minimal, so there is not much data to analyse. Later times grow more complex. There is shifting cultivation and then permanent settlements. Further in time, we see the rise of villages and then urban centres. With urban living, as in Harappan sites, archaeological data increases. Urban centres coincide at times with early writing, such as the Brahmi script, and perhaps record-keeping. Analysing the artefacts of economic exchange—their trade, their uses and their evolution—becomes crucial to understanding these societies.

Today the historian has also to understand how environmental changes influenced history. This is what draws in not only the history of landscapes and the changes manifest in a region but, more importantly, how environmental change affected human societies. When fertile areas gave way to deserts or when rivers changed course, people had to move and establish new settlements in places more conducive to better living. And so migration became a major concern as a driver of historical change. Migration in turn affected the interface of human settlements, the study of which may require the historian to consult genetic data if available. Inevitably, in understanding the human context, evidence from linguistic, environmental, geological, geographic and social sources can be crucial. Data from these and other relevant disciplines can be gathered and integrated by the historian, and/or these disciplines may suggest the kind of questions that they may ask. When historians now speak of the need to use interdisciplinary studies, this is what they mean. Comparative studies can suggest the themes to be investigated and the questions that can be asked of the sources. Writers of popular history are typically unaware of the centrality of these concerns. The historian's perspective has to be wide ranging. Merely listing dates, events and isolated facts is not sufficient.

NAMIT: Yes, the environment and its shaping of human societies is now central to historical understanding. Some now describe civilization itself as 'a gift' of the stable climate of the Holocene. Scholars are also urgently exploring the flip side of it: how humans, in turn, have radically altered the planet's ecology, producing our catastrophic climate change and mass extinctions. This is driving a critical re-evaluation of so much we have not yet questioned, or have brushed under the carpet, namely, the ecological and associated human costs of state societies, empires, colonialism, industrial modernity, capitalism and more. A good recent example of such work is Yale historian Sunil Amrith's *The Burning Earth: A History*. Another voice in this arena is Usha Alexander, whose columns in The Wire and 3 Quarks Daily look at societies through the lens of their various environmental attitudes. How have their worldviews impacted their ability to live in balance with nature? What ideas—or blind spots—may have hastened their decline? And what can we learn from them as we brace for the rapid and unsettling ecological changes coming at us fast?

There are also some focused lenses of socio-economic and cultural histories that have emerged more recently, including what are called caste studies, women's studies, religious studies and postcolonial studies. They are driven by new questions and draw on a different mix of sources and data from a variety of other disciplines that are relevant for answering those questions. How do you look at these focused new studies?

ROMILA: With caste and women's studies, it wasn't simply a matter of adding their histories to the existing framework of social history. Rather, it involved showing how these specific histories fundamentally altered the broader narrative of social history itself. Their integration has not only expanded the scope of social history but has also deepened our understanding of society by highlighting previously marginalized perspectives.

Dalit studies, in particular, have brought attention to communities historically marginalized as 'untouchables'. In our time, this field owes much to the pioneering efforts of Bhimrao Ramji Ambedkar, who strongly advocated such scholarship and made notable contributions to it himself. Today, Dalit studies explores various dimensions of Dalit life—often led by Dalit scholars—and examines their interactions with non-Dalit communities. We now also have growing interest in the study of adivasi experiences. As a result, history is no longer a study of mainly upper-caste society; it is increasingly attentive to the lives and contributions of all segments of society.

Women's studies, which emerged around the same time, moved beyond viewing women as a single, uniform category defined solely by gender. Instead, it emphasized the diverse experiences of women shaped by caste, class, religion, region and other social factors. Indian women historians and sociologists led this shift in perspective. No longer seen as a homogenous group, women came to be understood through their intersecting identities and lived realities—each shaped by distinct roles, activities and interests.

Historians also draw on the discipline of religious studies, which takes a different approach to religion than that of laypeople. For the latter, religion is mostly a matter of personal beliefs, shaped by stories, rituals and faith. Historians, however, see religious beliefs, stories and rituals as expressions of the social and emotional life of a community—reflecting its hopes, anxieties and lived experiences. They analyse these elements alongside the institutional and organizational aspects of religion, treating them as vital clues to understanding the society in which they operate. This viewpoint might not concern the lay individual believer, but it is crucial for constructing a meaningful account of a society's history.

Part of the issue is that religious believers often see their beliefs and rituals as timeless and unchanging. Their feeling of continuity—more justifiable perhaps in the Abrahamic religions—can obscure how much religious practice actually evolves over time. Historians, by contrast, are attentive to these shifts and seek to explain them. For instance, although Vedic religion continued to be practised by Brahmins, its social and economic context changed significantly in post-Vedic times. Its influence on the rest of 'Hindu society' diminished as new deities came to the forefront and new ritual practices evolved. Worship thus moved away from the non-iconic *yajna*s (sacred fire rituals) of the Vedic era—conducted at open-air altars—towards the temple-based, image-centred worship of deities such as Shiva, Vishnu and the goddesses of the Shakta traditions.

Historians seek to explain the reasons behind the emergence of this new form, called Puranic Hinduism—a form of religion shaped by the Puranas, the texts associated with this transformation. Their reasons for this change lie not in the teachings of individual preachers but in the practices of various social groups and sects, although the individual assumes more importance in the Shramana traditions—Buddhism, Jainism and the Ajivika faith, to which some add the Charvakas—as well as in the Bhakti form of Hinduism. Bhakti, in particular, marks a departure from earlier forms of religion by introducing new incarnations of deities and placing greater emphasis on the personal choice of the worshipper and the preacher. It embraces a variety of beliefs and rituals, mostly rooted in local and regional cultures—a notable shift from the more uniform rituals of Vedic and Puranic traditions. The historian of religion is especially interested in understanding why these changes occurred and how they affected the wider society.

NAMIT: Okay, allow me to do a little recap. So far we've talked about colonial history and its impact on the Indian imagination. We've discussed the historical method and how to approach various historiographies. We've seen how scholars of history sometimes reach divergent interpretations and conclusions, and how that's in the nature of the discipline itself—its Rashomon-like quality, as you memorably said. We've looked at the importance of interdisciplinary history in scholarship today.

I also heard you say, at least between the lines, that what unites scholars of history—or *should* unite them—is respect for authentic sources, high standards of evidence and clearly reasoned accounts. Even when they disagree, scholars are expected to ground their arguments in empirical evidence and clear reasoning. Such disagreements are often productive: they refine historical understanding and underline the multifarious nature of truth itself.

Now, this approach is fundamentally different from those who make up facts, wilfully misread sources, blur the lines between myth and history, lack interdisciplinary approaches, fail to argue rigorously and ignore reasoned critiques of their work. This is not how serious scholars of history typically operate. It makes a mockery of the historical method. Sadly, many popular history writers are doing this today, which has sown substantial confusion about history in the public sphere.

Okay, so let's now talk about how history is faring in the public realm.

The making [and consuming] of Mahua liquor by Kamuni Bai Baiga (2021). Baiga tribe of eastern MP. Courtesy: The Crites Collection.

7

What's Making Indian History Controversial in the Public Realm?

NAMIT: Most theorists of nationalism see history as a foundational element in the idea of a nation. They believe that nations need a shared sense of the past to foster social cohesion and solidarity, but we don't seem to have much of it today. Our public realm is in fact rife with bitter disagreements about our past—from the origins of the Indo-Aryans to the character of early Indian societies to the nature of Indo-Muslim rule to the role of caste and patriarchy in shaping Indian lives and much else.

I find three things that are interesting about Indian history: (1) That it is not really controversial within academia—i.e., in departments of history worldwide—at least not more so than any other region's academic history. It is 'controversial' mainly in the Indian public realm. (2) The disagreements we see are not the ordinary kind that one might expect between academic and popular discourses in any society. Our disagreements often contain entirely opposed or parallel narratives between academic and popular histories, as for instance on the Aryan question. This contrast is rather striking. (3) The hostility to academic history in India largely springs from a particular ecosystem and its cluster of feelings. It mainly comes from people with little training or knowledge or understanding of historical research, and they mostly happen to be Hindu nationalists of various stripes. All of this seems to me plainly true.

This ecosystem alleges that historians have 'betrayed us', claiming that a cabal of 'Marxist historians' controls academic discourse on Indian history both in India and abroad. According to this view, such scholars have denigrated Hindu culture and denied it its rightful place in the sun—all while going easy on Islamic culture and whitewashing the violence of 'Mughals' against Hindus. Largely led by non-academic history writers, this ecosystem feels wronged by the academic establishment and seeks to 'correct' and rewrite history to soothe its grievances. How did so many people start thinking this way in recent decades?

ROMILA: Perhaps they still think of history as origin myths and the narratives that legitimize the community they belong to—that's where we came from, that's who we are, etc. Identity explanations. And they don't appreciate the fact that there are contradictions in most investigations and analyses. And you have to understand why the contradictions exist, what they are, what they mean and how you relate to them. Now, it's fine if they believe in their own story of the past. Go ahead, but don't call it history.

The academic historian is simply saying, write what you like, believe what you like. Just don't call it history. If you're going to call it history, then follow the rules. You can't write history without following the rules and principles of the historical method. And this is really what is upsetting some people because the rules are tough. They're not easy. They are demanding. You really have to be very well trained to follow the historical method. It's not like it was in the old days, when any educated person could write what passed for history. Today, one must engage with prior scholarship on a topic and draw on proven evidence and careful analysis. This requires training and therefore it is not enough to be able to just read texts that come from the past and reproduce what they say. History has to be understood as being a segment of knowledge.

And this is part of the problem. Even a generation ago—and, indeed, even today—people read a dozen books, write one of their own, and proclaim themselves historians. This simply won't do. Becoming a historian requires rigorous training, disciplined thinking, and testing. You can't just bypass these steps and declare yourself a historian.

Lately, with all the hostility and interference, academic historians of quality are beginning to withdraw and become little islands of their own. This is most unfortunate, because society ought to intermingle with them and understand how they are explaining the world. Currently, the fear is that there will be two histories: pop history and academic history. That's not such a good idea if history is to help in understanding the past.

NAMIT: I think you're right. At one level, it is intriguing that most educated Indians don't seem to resist scientific knowledge per se, like Darwinian evolution, which many Christians in America resist. Indians are not the worst offenders on *that* front. Yet, they react so badly against *historical* knowledge. Why do you think that is?

ROMILA: We Indians don't resist scientific knowledge because many among us don't quite follow what it is saying or have simply not read it. How many educated Indians can see the implications of Darwin's views for understanding ourselves and our society? Or for that matter, the much-discussed American historian and philosopher of science Thomas Kuhn? If you scratch the surface, you'll find that many of us imagine Vishnu's ten incarnations and the principle of karma as anticipating Darwin's theory, which is then touted as evidence of Hinduism being the 'most scientific religion' in the world!

And why do we react badly against historical knowledge? Is it because we have a certain vision of ourselves, as being a particular people, as knowing what we identify with and what's meaningful in our lives? We don't understand that everybody has such a vision, and the other person has as much right to their vision as we have to ours. But when we insist that our vision is the correct one, that this is the way it was, then we have to prove it. We could just keep our vision to ourselves, but the moment we say, it's not just my vision, it's the right vision, and everybody has to believe in it because it is the correct vision, then we have to prove it. And that's where the conflict with the academic historian comes in.

NAMIT: Right. Actually, we do have Indians who resist Darwin. A few years ago, none other than India's Minister of State for Education had a brainwave. Darwin's theory of evolution is scientifically wrong, he declared, and should not be taught in school. It's wrong because no one, including our ancestors, has ever claimed to have seen an ape turning into a man. Imagine! He not only kept his job then, he is now the chancellor of a university!

What do you think are the roots of their resentment against historians? Does it begin with the nineteenth-century Hindu revivalist movement, which partly arose in reaction to colonial scholars, who were seen as denigrating India's past and its traditions? What experiences shape the Hindu nationalists' belief that mainstream history hasn't been fair to them?

ROMILA: You see, if you believe you've been denigrated, you cannot just turn around and abuse your denigrator. You have to prove to the world that the denigrator is wrong. That is what academic historians have done with various colonial accounts of our past. Likewise, if the academic historian is seen as denigrating popular history today, your reaction should not be to abuse the academic. Your reaction should be to say, I'm going to prove you wrong, and this is my evidence, and these are my reasons. You cannot get away by saying that what the academics say is not correct and then leave it at that. You've got to show them to be incorrect. And the proof must be not just your wishful thinking but evidence that is reliable and its interpretation that is transparent and accepted as such.

Take the story about the origin of the Indo-Aryans. The academic generally supports the idea that they migrated into northern India, but most popular history writers argue against this and say that the Indo-Aryans are indigenous to India. The popular version is that they are local. There isn't the evidence to support this theory, but they still insist on it. They claim that the academic view is an attack on Hinduism and on Hindus because it maintains that Hindu cultural roots are not entirely indigenous, that Hindus are a mixed people, deriving some ancestry from migrants who came from Central Asia.

This is a present-day crisis. Communities are competing for a position of superiority and some groups of Hindus are using majoritarianism of numbers and status in history to support their claim. It is partly motivated by that section of the Hindu middle class that wants to be seen as superior to all others, and it is not being conceded that status. Others are arguing that we don't want people differentiated by a claim to superiority. We've had enough of that. Everybody is equal in a democracy. The attitude of the former shows an inability to come to terms with a changing society, where people are not automatically ranked by caste but are treated as equal in status. So the intention is to obstruct that change by saying that the past is telling us something different. But the past is not telling us something different. These people are simply making up that past.

NAMIT: Yes. They also dislike historians discussing topics such as caste and patriarchy in our past. It makes them feel, umm, bad about themselves. But can India's past, or even its present, be understood without discussing such realities? Will banishing such discussions make these problems go away? Rather than looking into the mirror of history and reflecting, their reflex is to shatter the mirror—or silence those who hold it up. They expect historians to focus on flaunting the 'greatness' of their imagined community's past. Upper-caste Hindus now claim a thousand years of victimization by Muslims but hate to be reminded of the real domination and exploitation they visited on Dalits and adivasis for over two millennia, not to mention on women in their own communities.

The reality is that history in our public realm has become a tool for competition and scoring points, rather than a pursuit of deeper understanding and self-awareness. Hindutva narratives have little support among scholars, but they're still popular with many segments of the public, particularly their ethno-nationalist refrain of 'we, the once-glorious Hindus, are victims of history and "Marxist historians"'.

Doesn't this suggest a reactionary backlash because they don't like what they're hearing from historians, and the way it interferes with their cherished self-perception?

ROMILA: It interferes with their self-perception, and what puzzles me is that once we had a strong democratic national movement that was all-inclusive, and there were two relatively smaller religious nationalisms. One religious nationalism succeeded in Pakistan. The other one is busy trying to create a Hindu Rashtra. Why did religious nationalism become more powerful than the all-inclusive democratic nationalism? This is a crisis of this period. It's not a crisis of history. It's current politics.

NAMIT: It is a crisis, though I sometimes feel it's a byproduct of modernity itself. After all, the idea of representational politics only emerged in the modern era, and with it came candidates seeking votes from 'we the people'. As political consciousness grew, more citizens realized the power of their vote. This naturally intensified competition for political power, prompting some candidates to appeal to the social identities that people lean on to distinguish themselves from others. In a religious society like ours, religion can be turned into a basis of identity-based politics. Likewise with caste, which also happens to be a major fault line of inequality and discrimination. Resisting the lure of identity politics required a politically mature culture, ideally shaped by responsible social elites but who sadly remained few and far between. So such a culture didn't quite develop in India.

During the colonial period, the overarching unifying cause was to expel the British, and people rallied around it. But once that goal was achieved, I think the competitive logic of electoral democracy—especially in a society like ours, with its ascriptive divisions, deep-rooted inequalities and manufactured historical animosities—has produced the very crisis you speak of. This crisis may well be intrinsic to democracy itself. Or at least to political democracy built on pervasively anti-democratic substrates of social and economic life.

ROMILA: So, then really it is very much a product of the twentieth century.

NAMIT: Yeah. There are many positive things about democracy, but this unpleasant outcome too may be inherent to its logic. It's something, you know, that we have to guard against. I see it as a huge risk, a landmine of sorts, that's built into the modern enterprise.

ROMILA: (nods in agreement.)

The story of the snake god, Gond painting by Durgabai Vyam. Source: StoryLtd.com

8

The Colonialist Pillars of Hindutva History

NAMIT: Let's now take a closer look at the Hindutva view of history and its roots—psychological, intellectual and others. As you noted earlier, much of our early historical self-awareness was mediated through the colonial gaze and its construction of India's past. I think a major aspect of colonial history's legacy is that we Indians began understanding ourselves through the colonizers' eyes, using their concepts, categories and judgments. For over a century, this mental colonization coloured knowledge production in and about India, including our understanding of our past, as you noted a while ago.

But post-Independence, academic historians working on India have more consciously tried to decolonize historical scholarship, relying on the historical method to question colonial interpretations. You've done this too, since at least your Sardar Patel Memorial Lectures delivered in 1972 over All India Radio, published later as *The Past and Prejudice*. This process only gained steam after Edward Said's seminal book *Orientalism* (1978).

So it's ironic that Hindutva ideologues accuse mainstream historians of still being in the grip of colonial historiography while offering Hindutva as the pathway to decolonization. This view has been popularized by authors such as J. Sai Deepak and others, and it has gained momentum. Never mind that Hindutva itself is a form of internal colonization! It aspires to cultural hegemony and social domination over the many diverse and distinct traditions of India. Its ideologues have openly called for 'One Nation, One Culture', and we all know that their reference point is upper-caste Hindu culture. In fact, they don't have any examined or principled opposition to colonialism at all—just look at their marginal role in India's anti-colonial movement and their open admiration today for Israel's settler-colonialism in Palestine. How do you position the Hindutva world view in relation to the colonial school of Indian history?

ROMILA: When I trace the origins of Hindutva ideology, I see two roots. The first is the subconscious association and appropriation of the colonial view of Indian history, which includes the two strands I mentioned earlier: the two-nation theory of Mill and other colonial writers, which supposedly explained the structure of Indian society, and the other strand that sees Indian religion and culture beginning with the Aryans and the Vedas, rather than with the Harappans and the other pre-Indo-Aryan societies in the subcontinent.

The second root of Hindutva ideology is something we don't mention often enough, which is the more subtle imprint of European fascism. This pertains to Hindutva's political role in Indian society which has in this last decade become substantial. The leaders of the Rashtriya Swayamsevak Sangh (RSS) and creators of Hindutva—like Golwalkar, Moonje, Hedgewar, Savarkar—they all deeply admired Mussolini and Nazi Germany. For the latter, the progress of society in majoritarian terms meant that smaller groups such as the Gypsies and the Jews had to be removed. Much of this 'clearing up' was justified through notions of racial purity and strength, and the need to destroy the internal enemy that obstructs majoritarianism. We don't pay enough attention to what went into the making of the Hindutva ideology and its practice.[3]

One problem they faced as they conceived their majoritarian project was that it required a Hinduism that had to be much more uniform than it was. And that's what Hindutva has tried to do: to channel the sects, and diversity, into a monotheistic religion. It's very much inspired by the particular kind of European nationalism of the 1930s, which is why I call it 'Syndicated Hinduism'. Their idea of religion is not the same as historical Hinduism. So that's something we have to think about because religion now plays a significant political role.

NAMIT: Yes, European hyper-nationalism of the early twentieth century is an important example of what Hindu nationalists have learned and indigenized from colonial powers. Another colonial trick they've learned is that of divide-and-rule on religious grounds.

I also want to note that their attempt to reshape Hinduism was deeply inspired by its colonial framing. Taking cues from the religion of their overlords, early Hindu revivalists and nationalists set out to recast Hinduism into a monotheistic mould based on what they called 'classical Hinduism'—imagined around a textual canon with a leading holy book (the Gita), the abstract universal God (Brahman), a Vatican-like apex temple site at Ayodhya, standardized rituals, fewer deities and so on. In the process, and again echoing colonial attitudes, they too looked down on the 'degenerate polytheism' of folk religion.

What's interesting to me is that this new framing of 'Hinduism' was a joint project of upper-caste Hindus and colonial scholars, who characterized all of Hinduism as defined by the practices of its elite groups. All other traditions—of adivasis, subaltern castes, nomadic pastoral groups, etc.—got mauled by this new hegemonic conception of Hinduism. So this broad new construction of Hinduism, in which elite registers of Hinduism colonize and eclipse the smaller traditions, is also a legacy of the colonial period, no?

ROMILA: It is a colonial legacy. Because prior to the colonial construction of Hinduism, it wasn't a monotheistic religion. The pattern was the juxtaposition of diverse sects. If you stopped following a sect, you could start teaching and preaching and creating a new sect. Hinduism was a collection of sects, which gave it a certain variability and flexibility, and made it unusually different from Semitic religions. If you look at the texts of the precolonial period, people rarely describe themselves as being Hindu but as belonging to a particular sect. Major sects such as Vaishnava, Shaiva, Shakta—each with many sub-sects—but also smaller sects such as Nath Panthis, Kabir Panthis, Ganapatyas, Saurya, Dadu Panthis, Varkari and many others. They might partly overlap in their beliefs but could also be distant from each other.

Subsequent to the colonial construction, attempts were made to give it a monotheistic format, but it was not entirely successful. Attempts were made in the nineteenth century, including a few through organizations referred to as *samaja*s, but there was no equivalent to the Abrahamic religions. In a curious kind of way, the *dhamma* of the Buddha was in some ways organizationally closer to monotheism, except of course that there was no deity. But the question of whether or not Hinduism was a monotheistic religion has hovered over those trying to study or to reorganize the religion. The latest attempt is to try and base it on Hindutva ideology, but this has not yet succeeded.

Painting for the worship of deity at the time of labour pain of a woman, Saora Tribe.A panel at the Tribal Museum, Koraput, Odisha. Photo: Namit Arora.

9

Exploring a Possible Inferiority Complex

NAMIT: Now, it's true that Hindutva-like religious nationalism also exists in other parts of the world—as in Zionism, Islamism, White Christian nationalism in the USA and Europe, Buddhist nationalism in Sri Lanka and Burma and so on. But despite their many shared features, Hindutva also differs from them. I think some of the differences stem from a deeply internalized cultural inferiority complex among middle-class Hindus, which I'd like to explore here. Scholars such as Ashis Nandy, Christophe Jaffrelot and Partha Chatterjee have explored this complex as partly a consequence of colonialism.[4] I feel it is widespread enough and it helps create a large audience for Hindutva interpretations.

Among Hindu nationalists, this inferiority complex shows up in at least three ways: (1) Their warped sense of historical victimization and humiliation leads them to scapegoat and manufacture resentments against religious minorities, notably Muslims. (2) They cope with the inferiority complex by projecting superiority over everyone else, inventing or inflating achievements of a distant Hindu past. This surfaces in absurd claims of aircraft in prehistoric times, quantum physics in the Vedas, Sanskrit as the mother of all languages and countless other supposed triumphs—scientific, spiritual and cultural. (3) They seek external validation, as in getting Western scholars and institutions to recognize the amazing glory of Hindu civilization, mining out-of-context quotes from the likes of Will Durant, Mark Twain, Max Müller, Einstein, Voltaire …

ROMILA: They have to, in order to raise the levels of past achievements. They have to claim that the Hindu/Indian past was superior even to the current achievements of the West, the powers that colonized us. This is part of the mythology that believes in an absolutely brilliant past, far ahead of the rest of the world.

NAMIT: And they fabricate and exaggerate stories of victimization, that they were victimized en masse and their glorious civilization was destroyed by outsiders.

ROMILA: 'Infiltrators' in the current usage.

NAMIT: And Hindutva ideologues glorify and take immense pride in those who resisted these 'infiltrators'. Their world view is dominated by a rigid ingroup–outgroup mentality, framed largely in religious terms. In their pursuit of manufacturing Hindu pride, they even go as far as rewriting the outcomes of historical battles! Constructing a glorified Hindu past seems to serve a deep psychological need. But honestly, it's such a juvenile way of engaging with history!

What, in your view, are some reasons for this deep inferiority complex in the modern Hindu psyche, with its internalized sense of inadequacy and shame? I'm curious because it makes so many Hindus vulnerable to Hindutva storytelling—its compensatory bravado, bluster and muscular posturing. While the Hindutva worldview is driven by a small cadre of ideologues who weaponize religion for political gain, it now resonates widely with middle-class Hindus. They respond enthusiastically to its feel-good myths and the aggressive new Hinduism

championed by Prime Minister Narendra Modi and the Sangh Parivar. Modi understands their cultural inferiority complex and speaks directly to it—offering slogans like Vishwa Guru and Viksit Bharat. Such bromides have been central to his appeal, partly helping mask his failures of governance.
But where does this inferiority complex really come from? Has it been building up over a long period of time?

ROMILA: I don't think so. A cultural inferiority complex has to be measured against or compete with a superior culture. In the past, I don't know of any Indian culture conceding that another culture, local or distant, was distinctly superior. Every new culture that came in with migrants, traders, armies or whatever, came and settled in the Indian subcontinent and became a part of Indian culture. The interface with the locals did make it different from region to region but no single one was acknowledged by all the others as superior to them. This was not new. Knowledge in India related to mathematics and the proto sciences had been circulating in the then known world over the centuries. Unfortunately, this branch of knowledge has not been properly integrated into Indian history, so we seem not to ask for illumination on how it interfaced with other patterns of culture. This is crying out to be done. Let's not forget that during the Mughal period prior to the coming of the Europeans, the Indian economy seems to have been more successful than that of the countries with which it traded. It was an incredibly wealthy empire, hence the mind-blowing luxuries embedded in the style of elite living. Mathematics and technologies were exchanged as part of the regular scholarly interactions across Asia. Indian scholars and their work, which could perhaps be called proto science, drew much attention from other Asian scholars.

The nineteenth century saw something of a reversal in the fortunes of Asia vis-à-vis Europe. Asia's economic status did not remain as high as before. It could have been that its resources and their organization declined and at the same time Europe was able to mobilize new resources as well as considerably improve its technological knowledge and practice, and thus gain a dominant position. The Industrial Revolution introduced a new technology that vastly improved production in Europe and colonialism brought the raw material that was needed for this new technology to be much more productive than before. Indigenous Indian technologies seem not to have been improved upon to compete with the European equivalents, so they too tended to get left behind. So far the discussion on Asia and Europe in this period has been largely about their respective economic status, but it would also be worth examining the role of technology in economic production.

Associated with the decline is the fact that on previous occasions when new people migrated into and settled in India, whatever wealth they created, they ploughed it back into India and there was a turnover of resources and patterns of life. The conquerors settled in India. But with colonialism the colony was denuded of wealth-producing resources, poverty increased and little was done to create patterns of culture that were conducive to greater prosperity all round. There was the constant supervision of an alien people who regarded Indians as inferior. This was sought to be justified by theories of race, claimed as knowledge, and which underlined the theory of inferiority of the Indian. The consistent repetition of inferiority did the damage. The imposition of a new technology introduced by the colonial power not only set aside the traditional Indian systems of knowledge, but these also tended to get dismissed in the general admiration of the technology from the West.

The two-nation theory also had a role in these changes. During the Mughal period, there was interest in and praise for traditional culture, such as the philosophical and religious dialogues, the Bhakti and Sufi traditions, the evolution of schools of music, literature and language and suchlike. Indian mathematical knowledge, for instance, had been treated with much respect by scholars from the Arab world, yet now these received little attention. But the colonial notion of two nations in conflict was a disaster because one was said to dominate over the other and the two were projected as inferior to the British who regarded themselves as holding the balance. The colonials were concerned with all kinds of domination that would, above all, enable them to control the economy. It was beyond their comprehension that someone like Akbar, in a sense, transcended the two religious traditions, engaging in innovative religious thought in his search for a new faith. The colonial understanding was limited to seeing the situation only as Muslim domination. Then, after colonial assessments portrayed Muslim culture as inferior, it created an added sense of embarrassment to Hindus for having been ruled by a culture deemed inferior in their framework.

NAMIT: Many colonial influences on history writing have been damaging indeed, as you noted earlier. The colonials followed that up with frequent suggestions of the inferiority of Indians, which they imagined as the cause of the social backwardness they saw in sundry practices of caste, gender and popular religion. The colonials saw Indians as racially inferior, indolent and incapable of self-rule. It's true that a few colonials did appreciate aspects of Indian culture, but by and large, they devalued Indian art, literature, religion and aesthetics. They glibly denigrated Indian languages as crude and unfit for 'proper education'. So yes, this colonial encounter did significant damage to the self-esteem of many upper-caste Hindus, who had long seen themselves as superior. Even post-Independence, this wasn't helped by Western stereotypes of India as a godforsaken land of snake charmers, crushing poverty and rank superstitions.

I wonder how much of the upper-caste Hindu inferiority complex stems from the realization that modern knowledge systems have displaced and rendered many traditional ones obsolete—especially those rooted in the Brahmanical substrate. Ayurveda and Vastu Shastra, for instance, are now rightly regarded as pseudo-sciences. Among many modern Hindu elites, this seems to have produced a lingering sense of 'we have lost out', that if modernity—with its knowledge systems and values and notions of 'progress' and 'development'—is the ruling game in town, then we have everything to learn from the West, while the world has little to learn from us, apart from a handful of soft cultural exports like yoga, spicy food, some music and traditional handicrafts.

And this sense of 'defeat'—especially in a scientific-technological sense, which is the ultimate yardstick of the modern world and its big source of power—created a search for explanations. This search, far from provoking honest self-reflection, has led a significant section of Hindu elites to look for scapegoats. And the easy targets of blame become the Muslims and the colonial rulers. They destroyed our greatness, we are told. Before 'the Mughals'—a catch-all term for all Indo-Muslim rulers—invaded and enslaved us, Hindus were prosperous, had great cities, flourishing science, technology, medicine, universities and a harmonious society. Women were held in high regard, Brahmins spread their love of learning and lived spartan lives, and caste was fluid and based on aptitude—feel-good stories with a slim basis in reality. Alongside, the same Hindu elites vastly overestimate India's intellectual relevance in today's world, which shows up in their cringe Vishwa Guru propaganda. Very little critical reflection is undertaken to try and understand one's own culture as it really was—and is—with both its inadequacies and its upsides.

ROMILA: I think that is true to some extent and it did contribute to the general perception. There was little attention given initially to investigating knowledge systems other than what the British held. This was assumed to be the only viable one and all others judged by it. You know, what's curious to me is that even today, our interest in the achievements of ancient Indians seems to be only skin deep. Why is there so little serious interest in investigating early Indian proto-scientific knowledge? By this I mean not just describing what was discovered, but analysing what the early scholars investigated and why, how they arrived at their conclusions, and how they used this knowledge to advance the technology of their times. Such fundamental questions remain unanswered. The systems involved in the production of this knowledge—however it is rated—have to be studied. Such a study in terms of analysing what is scientific about this knowledge and what is not, should be familiar to students.

As a contrast to this, let me mention an institute in Cambridge founded by Joseph Needham (1900–95), the English scholar of the history of Chinese science. It has published many volumes of quality research on traditional Chinese scientific knowledge. That's not happening here. We keep talking about our scientific achievements. Which institute in India has produced a reliable multi-volume history of the sciences in pre-modern India?

In a way, we're not taking ourselves seriously. We're going on nurturing our resentment, complaining about how we were looked down upon, denigrated, victimized. In truth, we're still looking down on ourselves. We should be examining our inheritance in a more serious, reliable way. Let me give you a personal example. The one major aspect of historical study that I have been obsessive about throughout my life and on which I finally wrote a stout volume, was historiography—the study of the writing of history by historians. My interest was drawn to it in the late 1950s, when it was commonly said that the Indians of earlier times lacked a sense of history and therefore wrote no history—unlike the ancient Greeks and the Chinese who wrote history. I could also have said either that there was a sense of history and quoted mythology—as some popular writers are doing today, or I could have set it aside and said that Indians were not interested in the past. But I decided to investigate what the interest in the past could have been and how was it given shape—a shape different from what the Greeks and Chinese gave it, but nevertheless worth investigating and discussing. Such investigations inevitably reveal new aspects of the culture of a society, and this is valuable.

NAMIT: Yes, how I wish I had a course in the history of Indian science and technology in college. In terms of research, we do have Debiprasad Chattopadhyaya's *History of Science and Technology in Ancient India* (1986–96). More recently, historian of science Meera Nanda has illuminated some aspects of it too. Still, I agree that Indians have not done enough secular research in this area, or at least not prioritized disseminating or teaching it effectively to undergraduates and the public. That remains a significant drawback.

And even our yardsticks, shaped by colonial modernity, have long resisted looking at our cultural inheritance and knowledge systems associated with the non-elite sections of society, such as the ecological practices of adivasis. Or take the passive cooling structures that medieval Indian architects designed to regulate interior temperatures—how well do we understand them? Instead, some of us have been busy mythologizing ancient Indian techno-scientific achievements and basking in their fictional glory. I vaguely recall this joke I came across on social media: instead of striving to produce the best mathematics, literature and science in India today, Hindu hyper-nationalists spend all their time insisting that 5000 years ago their ancestors did the best mathematics, literature and science (laughs).

A Sohrai wall painting from Mithila, Jharkhand, by Pratha Bopche (public domain). The artform is mainly practised by women of the community, and their paintings use pigments sourced from nature.

10

Scientific and Historical Temper among Educated Indians

NAMIT: I believe another reason why history has so easily become controversial in India is the pervasive lack of 'historical temper' among our educated elites. Just as 'scientific temper' implies a good sense of physical reality among people, 'historical temper' implies a good sense of historical reality. A society with scientific temper will resist pseudo-sciences such as astrology, homeopathy, much of Ayurveda, Vastu Shastra and the miracle of Ganesh statues drinking milk. It won't elevate mystical charlatans and spiritual conmen. Likewise, a society with historical temper will resist myths and fantasies peddled as history and won't fall for conspiracy theories. More of its prominent men and women would display critical thinking on questions about our past. They would know that there is no evidence to establish Rama as a historical figure; that epic literature like the Mahabharata was never meant to be a chronicle of actual events but rather evolved as imaginative cultural stories, shaped and retold by charioteer bards and others to entertain and inspire their audiences.

It seems to me that historical temper remains strikingly low among India's elite—especially among its engineers, lawyers, doctors, business majors and bureaucrats who dominate its civic and democratic institutions. Many of them, suave and articulate, are now at the forefront of propagating Hindutva storytelling via books, social media, podcasts, talk shows and slickly produced films. Within this ecosystem, a host of unfounded claims continue to circulate—for instance, that the Aryans were indigenous to India, that the Harappan Civilization was Vedic and spoke Sanskrit, or that Hindu scriptures anticipated many discoveries of modern science. Claims like these go on and on! There's the myth of a so-called 'Hindu genocide', alleging that Muslim invaders destroyed 60,000 temples and killed 80 million Hindus—more than the entire population of north India at the time! The sheer absurdity of such figures hasn't stopped Hindutva historians such as Vikram Sampath and others from amplifying them in mainstream forums.[5] Add to that the bogus alarm over India becoming a Muslim-majority state due to supposedly 'skyrocketing' Muslim birthrates—despite decades of data showing a steady decline and near convergence of Hindu and Muslim fertility rates. Or the ludicrous claim that the Taj Mahal was originally a Hindu temple. It reflects a truly mind-boggling world view—often patronized by those who are considered our 'best and brightest'!

And then these Hindutva historians complain about being shut out by an 'academic cabal' that refuses to take them seriously. But isn't this like science deniers lamenting their lack of recognition from science academies?

Given how crucial the cultivation of historical temper is to inclusive democratic societies, why do you think we have achieved so little in independent India, especially among the men and women of our professional classes?

ROMILA: It is perhaps more complicated. I think it comes from two things at least. One is that we, in modern times, have not given enough respect to rational, logical thinking as part of our philosophical tradition. We are basically rather disinterested in the Charvaka writing or the debates among philosophers in which rational arguments are a striking component. We have tended to ignore even our philosophical schools of the past that emphasized the importance of rationality or discussed dissenting ideas. The Brahmins of pre-modern times were well aware of this and had a term for those advancing such ideas. They were called *nastika*s, or the non-believers.

This is partly because we are obsessed with the idea that our culture was entirely spiritual and that this distinguished us from the West. But culture is always mixed. There is no lack of spirituality in early Western thinking and there is notable rationality in early Indian thinking. Madhavacharya, a fourteenth-century philosopher, opens his study of the various current philosophical schools with the Charvaka, not because he rates it as the best but because there is apparently interest in it. It is listed as a significant school of philosophy. Today such philosophical thinking would tend to be described as alien and not indigenous.

The lacuna among Indian scientists is their seeming lack of interest in the social and intellectual context of science and technology, or what may be called the intellectual base of scientific thinking. They're all very busy with the technicalities and doing very well there but ask them what that means in social terms for society and the answer is often a blank. Now, if there was a changed approach to all knowledge, as I think is possible, middle-class India could have a greater awareness of the centrality of history in understanding society—both past and present. They would listen to historians talking about the relevance of history to society.

Instead, the government is busy cutting down the history syllabus, presuming that understanding the past is not so relevant. This is a limited view of not only history but of knowledge. It's the inability to understand the context of knowledge, which is absolutely fundamental to any advance. Also, we have to see the patterns by which knowledge has advanced in our culture. This is dependent on the sources we use and the questions we ask.

NAMIT: I think the point you made about the Charvakas and nastikas is spot on.

Yes, this government is not only cutting down academic history, it is also actively promoting pseudo-science through its AYUSH ministry. What's worrying is that even college-educated Indians are embracing it with enthusiasm. And we have this state of affairs despite the fact that we've had modern education for decades. Why does it still . . .

ROMILA: Wait, what kind of education have we really had? Yes, we've been taught some fragments of modern knowledge, but not in a way that enables us to understand its basic foundations. The big breakthroughs and advances in science are happening elsewhere, and we are largely imitating them. Have we even debated what of modern scientific knowledge we should give priority to and why? What have we wanted in seventy-five years? Has any major Indian invention come from knowledge generated within Indian institutions of research during this period?

But we cannot take this argument very far because we have to remember that this kind of knowledge does not get generated in only one place by a handful of people. It is frequently a culmination of the cross-fertilization of ideas. The history of this cross-fertilization is the significant issue that historians should be studying.

NAMIT: Yeah. Is the dismal state of affairs with respect to scientific temper and knowledge creation mainly because modern science as a practice, and as a way of thinking, came to us late, through our collision with Europe? And it still sits lightly on top and hasn't been assimilated enough—not even by our elites who have had the most exposure to it.

ROMILA: It hasn't been assimilated.

NAMIT: I reviewed this book a while ago, *The Caste of Merit* by Ajantha Subramanian, anthropologist and scholar of South Asia at Harvard. In it, she looks at the factors that attracted Indian elites to technical and scientific education during the colonial era. She shows that even when upper-caste Indians flocked to colonial-era schools to pursue English and modern education—and began vying for these new scientific and engineering jobs that were coming up in the colonial administration—their approach was instrumental. It was a means to power, to just gain the types of knowledge that would help them maintain their privileges and their superior status in society.

ROMILA: They didn't approach it as an investigation into knowledge.

NAMIT: Right. They approached it in a Brahmanical way! For instance, while studying mechanical and civil engineering, they avoided hands-on work. They absorbed theoretical knowledge in the classroom but, as British observers noted, often lacked the 'practical sense' and 'the grit and common sense which mark the engineer'. Manual labour was seen as beneath them—dignity of labour was alien to their world view. They attended colleges that preserved caste practices in the dining hall.

In other words, upper-caste Indians were drawn to the new science and engineering vocations mainly for their ability to provide financial security and the prestige of association with the colonial state, without internalizing the questioning spirit that goes with it.

ROMILA: Which is the way the colonials wanted it.

NAMIT: Yes, totally.

ROMILA: The colonials would have been very worried if Indians had said, now we're going to investigate this bit of knowledge that you're teaching us. But we didn't, we haven't thrown off that old habit of imitating the end product but not experimenting with how it came about.

NAMIT: Yes, this habit is old indeed! Even Alberuni had noticed it. Such is the state of things in India, he lamented a thousand years ago, that Brahmins attempt to combine ideas of purity with the pursuit of science. That narrow approach to knowledge—and its bookish, rote-learning modes, or 'learning by heart'—is still very much with us.

I wonder what can be done to change this. I mean, without an adequate level of scientific and historical temper, all bets are off for so many things in modern democracies—it's at least a necessary ingredient, if not a sufficient one. I see this lack in my peers from the IIT system. I see it even in the top tiers of professional achievers. And, you know, it looks bleak. Even our best institutes of science and technology impart very little critical thinking. They have no holistic idea of learning. It's mostly about imparting narrowly lucrative skills to get ahead in a rat race. Many of their graduates even acquire PhDs from famed universities, yet in so many ways continue to validate American physicist Richard Feynman's observation, 'you can have a PhD and still be an idiot.'

I think this partly goes down to our school system. When I was growing up, middle-class kids got herded into two streams: medicine and engineering. They got herded. If a kid showed more interest in history, civics, literature or the arts, others would whisper: 'see, he's clearly not bright enough for engineering and medicine! Otherwise, why would he choose anything else?' (laughs) With such a mercenary attitude, which still pervades our middle classes, is it surprising what we have today?

ROMILA: When I look at all the curricula the Ministry of Education is putting out for schools, and now even universities, I know that it needs greater attention in the form of more discussion and debate on what needs to be taught. There is no shortage of teachers who are willing to debate these decisions. But somehow more attention is given to the stream that will go into the technical sciences such as engineering, computers, medicine and that kind of thing. There is far less appreciation for social sciences. It's not understood that there is the human context to knowledge, that knowledge is tied to a human situation.

NAMIT: Yes, our pedagogy is in crisis. It has been so for a long time. And the current dispensation is further demoting humanities and social science education and research in universities. But then again, if this regime started raising funding for history, it could well be tied to legitimizing their version of history, for which they might staff history departments accordingly—more folks like Sita Ram Goel, P.N. Oak and the older K.S. Lal. So maybe it's good that this anti-intellectual dispensation is not raising funds for history (laughs).

More seriously, I think another reason why history has become so controversial is due to our government's meddling in history curriculums. History is, of course, central to all nationalist projects. But this regime's version of history very significantly diverges from the scholarly consensus. Various non-historians now control the contents of history textbooks. Their latest changes in NCERT texts cast doubt on the Indo-Aryan migrations and speak of a 'Sindhu-Saraswati civilization' when referring to the Harappans; they suppress discussion of the ills of the caste system, presumably to not hurt the delicate feelings of upper-caste folk; the Mughals alone are deemed 'brutal' and 'ruthless conquerors', giving a free pass to the Cholas, the Marathas and others; Nathuram Godse, Gandhi's murderer, is now just 'a young man', his ideological affiliations erased; the Gujarat pogroms of 2002 have been removed and so on.[6] Who can fail to see the motivations behind such changes?

Even at the IITs, they're propping up centres of 'Indian Knowledge Systems' led by Hindutva ideology, which are doling out pseudoscience to young minds.[7] It seems to me that a long-term consequence of such meddling with education is to produce citizens with an even greater deficit of historical temper and humanistic imagination.

You were once involved in the shaping of history curriculums for schools. And while it's true that all nationalist regimes support and promote certain historical interpretations over others, why is India's Hindu nationalist regime so obsessed with the control of history textbooks and shaping them in ways I have just described?

ROMILA: Well, I think those currently shaping the syllabus are driven by an obsession with mythologizing the past. For one thing, they reject serious, evidence-based history because it raises difficult questions—ethical, social and political—that challenge comforting narratives. It messes with their self-perceptions and cherished identities. Mythologizing the past allows them to say, 'It wasn't like that but like this,' and in doing so, they get to replace inconvenient truths with more palatable fictions.

Second, as I said earlier, the past is viewed as essential to legitimizing the present. In fact, all nationalisms the world over seek legitimacy from the past. So your past has to be made into something that will legitimize your goals in the present. It has to serve as a kind of justification for what you're doing politically today. Clearly, this is politicizing the past as well. That's really what Hindutva-dominated 'history' is about—politicizing the past. And it's a strong weapon in the hands of those that support it.

In effect, the regime is using its authority to dictate the kind of history that should be officially taught and endorsed. School textbooks are being extensively rewritten, and college and university curricula are being 'rationalized'—that's what they call this activity! Which really means stripping away the most intellectually and academically valuable parts of the syllabus. All of this serves their larger agenda of advancing their Hindu Rashtra. The irony is striking: Hindutva 'history' borrows heavily from outdated colonial interpretations—long discredited by serious scholars. The public must recognize what is truly at stake.

Art of the Warli tribe depicting a village scene with stylized figures, Maharashtra. Source: JioMart.

11

The Silence of the Academic Lambs

NAMIT: So we have a government that's hostile to critical thinking and is messing with history curricula. Alongside, we also have an army of Hindutva ideologues who've weaponized history to promote their chauvinistic vision of a Hindu nation. They're zealously producing 'content' that blurs the lines between myth and history—and this government actively supports them! They appeal to people's basest instincts of fear and resentment. They peddle fake history and lurid conspiracy theories on 'WhatsApp university'. They air their hostility to academic historians on social media and on traditional media captive to right-wing politics. They are patronized directly by our right-wing government, with funds, jobs, positions of influence, awards and access to power. So in this ecosystem, just about anything can be put out as 'history'.

I know you are very familiar with all this. But amid all this churn, I wonder where the academic historians are. Social activism used to be more common among historians of your generation. But today, with a handful of exceptions—you're still at it and a few others—the vast majority of academic historians seem to have gone quiet even as their discipline gets mauled. It's true that some have written books for general audiences but that's only one part of the challenge. The other crucial part I would like to discuss here is that too few historians are now stepping up to challenge fake history that's flooding our public arena. They seldom weigh in on conspiracy theories—about historical figures, events, or sites—that go viral and worsen communal strife. They rarely review bestselling popular history books and authors that are poisoning minds. There are now so many historical dramas on TV and film, but historians hardly review or offer assessments of their quality in mainstream forums.

Shouldn't more academic historians play a greater role in resisting and critiquing the appalling quality of popular history that's polluting the public sphere? What explains their substantial silence? And how might this change?

ROMILA: I wouldn't single out historians although they have greater reason to question popular theories. I think all academics in India need to participate, even if only marginally, in debates where their discipline is being tossed about. I think the silence today is partly explained by the fact that at one level, public opposition to them takes the form of virulent abuse—or even assassination in some cases as has happened in this past decade. And we all know how uncontrolled the abuse is.

At another level, there is a fear that for speaking out, they might get arrested and sent to jail for being 'anti-national' or held under UAPA for opposing the views of the government, for disagreeing with the latter's fake histories. That if they are seen as questioning the actions of the government, they will be labelled 'Urban Naxals' and punished.[8] So at one level, their preference for being silent is understandable. Nevertheless, I think it is possible to speak out without openly confronting the government organizations, it is possible to go on insisting that this is not history and explaining why. There isn't enough questioning of what's being claimed in popular history.

I mean, the interesting thing is that during the days of COVID-19, students, as part of a heritage exploration initiative called Karwaan, arranged for academics to give lectures on history on Zoom. The audiences went up to 30,000! So it is not that there is no interest in academic history or that academics cannot communicate with the general public. Interest in academic history is there. Social media is deliberately being used to exploit that interest but by converting it to push forward fake history because that is the only level of history that most social media consumers find acceptable and claim to understand. Or they're being served an unrecognizably watered-down academic history. Social media is failing to serve that segment in the middle class that would be quite interested in listening to a higher level of discourse. More importantly, if such discourse is nurtured by more such initiatives, how would it affect the way in which we see ourselves as Indians and understand an Indian past?

We tried introducing the idea of slightly more challenging programmes and discussion when I was in Prasar Bharati and suggested an education channel run by professional academics. It was shot down by the Bharatiya Janata Party in 1999, for obvious reasons. They claimed there was no money to finance such a channel and yet other channels were being established for entertaining the general public. We must also remember that such arguments apply to more than history when it comes to raising the standards in the teaching and reading of a subject. If the standards of education continue to be lowered, as is happening at the moment, people will not be interested in argument and discussion any longer. They will just take what comes. That may perhaps be the intention with regard to education.

NAMIT: Yeah, it's astonishing how little funding there is for quality programming in history or science on our TV channels—the kind one finds in the US, Europe and many Asian countries, on channels like the PBS, the BBC, Discovery, History, National Geographic, Toute l'Histoire, NHK World, etc.

They also have numerous foundations and trusts that fund the arts, public education, documentaries, museums, public lectures and more. These do so much to lubricate intellectual life and civic discourse in modern societies. Forget funds for quality programming and projects, we have a severe lack of public libraries in most of our towns and cities. That's a surefire way to ensure we never become a Vishwa Guru! Our museums, too, remain dull spaces with insipid and poorly curated displays—they never connect the dots to present the larger story and context.

So while our academics don't get opportunities for impactful public projects with a wide reach, today they aren't even participating where they can. Some do write accessible books for the general public, but in today's world, they should also be disseminating history through online lectures, videos, podcasts, articles, book reviews, talk shows and so on. As in many public universities abroad, our best teaching professors could record and host their entire course of lectures online for free. Further, best-selling Hindutva 'history' books keep coming out—they frequently outsell books by academics 10x or more—but our academic historians do not review them. Why are they silent? Academics, given their subject-matter expertise, ought to publicly discuss the problems with such texts that are influencing so many minds—of our younger engineers, lawyers, doctors, businessmen—people who will command institutional power and significantly shape our collective future. Academics could speak or write about such works in popular forums, or respond through YouTube videos, which can be made inexpensively. I think they will find an eager audience; the appetite for critical analysis is very much alive. It will make a difference.

ROMILA: I think it's again the fear of being abused. It is incredible that ever since the abuse started, in the time of the government after the Emergency, when the first demand was made that the textbooks we had written for the NCERT should be banned, there has been little attempt to express disagreement with us by writing well-researched counter views. There can hardly be any debate if one side has little or no knowledge of history. And what the trolls say about us in online forums, including the innuendos and the direct remarks about women, I find quite repelling. Is this what these trolls call Hindu culture? When it is sometimes brought to my attention and I read it, my reaction is that they need to see psychiatrists.

NAMIT: That's so true. I acknowledge that the fear is real. I feel it myself often enough. And the ultra-sexualized nature of online hostility is disturbing indeed. Indian trolls have an international reputation on that front. In this domain, we truly are Vishwa Gurus! I can only imagine how vulnerable women academics must feel, which is another reason I like this young historian, Ruchika Sharma. She is brave and combative. She publicly calls out and challenges popular writers of Hindutva history on social media. She also makes informative videos in Hindi about various historical episodes. You know, we need more of that.

ROMILA: If that is what she does, and it is effective in combatting fake history, we need more of that, you're absolutely right.

NAMIT: And I know that academics have a range of personal life situations and talents. Many are shy and introverted and loath to take on confrontational postures. Many contribute in less visible ways, such as in classrooms—quietly teaching credible history well. But many could do a lot more. Overall, and as a group, I think academics may be ceding far more ground to fear than is warranted today. It is one thing to challenge the government. They don't necessarily have to do that, as you said. They can also use tact and erudition to challenge these big influencers and their corrosive ideas. There is still room for that.

To be fair, academics do occasionally critique popular history that is very problematic. For instance, in the *Caravan*, historian Meera Visvanathan has dissected economist Sanjeev Sanyal's approach to historical writing.[9] She shows how Sanyal often begins with a litany of grievances about how India's history got hijacked by the colonials and 'cultural Marxists'. This tactic serves to rile up readers, framing him as a heroic figure reclaiming the 'correct history' of India from a supposedly compromised academy. From there, he takes significant liberties in interpreting legendary and contradictory sources—ones that academic historians typically avoid or handle with great caution due to their unreliability. But he reads them in amateurish and narrowly partisan ways that support his vision of Hindu nationalism.

Visvanathan cites Sanyal's writings on Ashoka, among other examples, but this pattern is evident throughout his work. Motivated misreadings are common. In his books, he claims that the Rig Veda was 'compiled in the third millennium BC', placing it during the mature phase of the Harappan Civilization! He refers to the depiction of horses in several cave paintings at Bhimbetka to suggest that humans used horses in the subcontinent long before the early second millennium BCE.[10] He does this to support his fond Hindutva belief, against all evidence, that the horse-riding Indo-Aryans were indigenous to the subcontinent and so were naturally coextensive with the Harappan Civilization. He conveniently omits something that scholars and avid readers of history have long known about these cave paintings, that they were created over many millennia, stretching from pre-Harappan neolithic times to the Common Era—which accounts for the depiction of horses. Such omissions and distortions often go unnoticed by his unknowing readers who are not students of history—and apparently even his editors. As Visvanathan notes, 'The success of Sanyal's books stems from a pervasive inability to understand historical expertise'. He continues to peddle his narratives 'because professional historians have never taken him seriously [and] he has never been contested or critiqued [by them].' Would it surprise anyone that he is now on a panel of experts tasked to rewrite NCERT social science textbooks?!

The problem is that reviews like Visvanathan's are rare today. The vast majority of academics remain silent, failing to push back against the tide of pseudo-history now being propagated, in no particular order, by figures like Rajiv Malhotra, Sanjeev Sanyal, Vikram Sampath, J. Sai Deepak, Abhijit Chavda, Raj Vedam, Nilesh Oak, Anand Ranganathan, Amish Tripathi, and numerous others, often translated in regional languages. Their work, as I see it, mostly represents varying combinations of half-truths, scholarly ineptitude and sectarian malice. Funnily, these popular writers hurl the same accusations against their academic opponents!

ROMILA: I know, but there's this other side to it which also needs to be looked at. Some of us have spent our lives divided between public issues and personal research. But I think more and more academics are just doing personal research and saying, *hum kyun phasaen usme* (why should I entangle myself with that)?

You see, the cumulative effect of all this—the so-called New Educational Policy, the removal of sections in history textbooks, state-sponsored disinformation and so on—is that we will produce a generation of ill-educated Indians. They will be ill-equipped to make original contributions in history, other forms of knowledge or much else. I fear that much of the most thoughtful scholarship on Indian history and culture—work that is generating fresh insights—will be sidelined or confined to academic circles. It's unlikely to reach a wider audience not because scholars are uninterested in public engagement but because such work is routinely misrepresented or attacked in public discourse. This may further erode the already limited public appetite for understanding history in its many dimensions. Ironically, nuanced histories will continue to be read and valued in centres of South Asian historical research abroad—even as they are marginalized at home.

NAMIT: You're right. And on a related note, let me add a clarification here. I very much think that it's not just the responsibility of academics to fight bad history in the public realm. I only feel that they need to do their part. The truth is that good history also matters to other sober members of society, many of whom are not lacking in critical thinking. Many brilliant non-academic history writers—public historians—are producing admirable 'public history', a genre that makes reliable history more accessible and engaging, bridging the gap between academic research and the public. These individuals are making a real difference not only by writing commendable and approachable books but especially by being vocal on social media, often in regional languages, which is where fake history is most active today. I'm thinking here, in no particular order, of people like Ram Puniyani, Ashok Kumar Pandey (of the Hindi YouTube channel, *The Credible History*), Anirudh Kanisetti, Manu S. Pillai, Tony Joseph, Shoaib Daniyal, Mini Menon, Sohail Hashmi, Rana Safvi, Ravish Kumar and more. Regional language spheres surely have their counterparts. I'm most familiar with English, where many plucky voices are pushing back against fake narratives—on independent media platforms like The Wire, Scroll.in and Alt News; in magazines like *Caravan* and *Himal Southasian*; on history websites like Indian History Collective, Storytrails and Live History India; and through podcasts, blogs, travel guidebooks, newspapers, small presses and other forums. That said, their public reach remains small compared to mainstream media—perhaps a big part of the reason they're allowed to exist by the powers that be.

Alright, so we've explored some reasons for why today's academic historians are perhaps not doing enough to push back against all the fake history that's being promoted. Fear of abuse and reprisals has led many to go silent, making them avoid even the safer pathways still open for resisting disinformation and defending their discipline.

This brings me to a different accusation often made against academic historians, which is that the very rise of fake history in India is due to the failure of academics to write accessibly for the general public. It is alleged that Indian academics have been living in ivory towers and revelling in their obscure language steeped in Marxist jargon, which then created a vacuum that was filled by 'WhatsApp history'—or pseudo, fake, make-believe history. The argument runs that Indian academics mostly just talk to each other and have done little to disseminate credible history to the average reader, which then has allowed pseudo-history to prosper. In other words, if only Indian academics had written about the greatness of Indian civilization in evocative prose, 'WhatsApp history' may not have come up at all. What are your thoughts on this line of attack on academic historians?

ROMILA: Such statements are really rather curious because in most societies, there isn't such an excessively sharp distinction between academic history and the narratives that dominate the public sphere. In most fields of knowledge, there is indeed some difference between the understanding of professional researchers and that of interested laypersons. There are publications of a highly specialized kind accessible only to those knowledgeable in that discipline. But there are also other publications that aim to present that knowledge in a manner that is comprehensible to the non-specialist. Such publications are generally not written by the professional specialist but by an intelligent middle-man as it were, who consults with the professional specialist, so that what is presented is authentic as far as possible. We need more such people not only with reference to history but to many forms of knowledge.

Obviously, there is something specific to the Indian situation that has resulted in this sharp division we have in writing history. Some people I've discussed this with think that this idea of academics being responsible for the divide is a pathetic argument. I tend to agree, since such statements can hardly stand scrutiny. The suggestion that academic history is not understood by the public because it uses a Marxist framework to explain the past is what some Hindutva followers also recite, though most of them have no clue as to what Marxism or Marxist historiography is. Since such statements are made frequently and casually, this needs further discussion.

I think there are at least two features specific to our society that are responsible for the rise of 'WhatsApp history' and neither has to do with academic historians. The first is our abysmally poor standard of education, as we were speaking about earlier. Even our so-called educated middle classes, more often than not, lack a basic understanding of any social science discipline. History is still widely seen as a collection of narratives about the past, not as a discipline that explains how societies functioned long ago, how they changed and so on. History is not understood, nor are economics and sociology. If these were better understood, we might have had a more thoughtful society. To make matters worse, educational standards keep falling and there comes a point when the decline is such that its usefulness tends to become an almost pointless enterprise. There is no emphasis on close reading, questioning and critical thinking, which is in fact what education involves. But our official system of education, which is what is widely adopted, is fast becoming one in which texts are treated as sources of catechism—all the questions and answers are given, and one just has to memorize them, without pausing to consider or debate their intrinsic meaning. Textbooks are mauled and courses are chopped up into unconnected, indigestible bits—the erasure of the Mughals, for example—and questioning is not encouraged. With so many structural barriers to teaching the subject well, I'm always amazed that some teachers still manage to get something across to the student, and that some students respond by asking further questions.

The second reason is that in our times, politics is impinging far more on our lives than ever before. Hindutva has a theory about the past that draws from texts on mythology, on the colonial view of Indian history and a believed fantasy history. This has to be learnt by heart and not questioned. Those who question it are dubbed Marxists, even if the answers they come up with are anything but Marxist. Many who claim to be educated and knowledgeable have no idea what Marxist means. Or for that matter, any other theory of explanation: Weberian, Foucauldian or even the 'cultural turn'. Hindutva has a vision for the future that is the Hindu Rashtra—a state controlled by majoritarian Hindu rule. The politicians of the Hindu Right need to construct a reliable history with a better claim to support their ambition of the Hindu Rashtra. It is not a coincidence that there is today in India a partiality towards communal thinking cultivated by the deliberate encouraging of certain attitudes towards 'the Other' that are hostile. This did not exist in pre-colonial times when there were small conflicts for a variety of reasons but not communal riots. A communal vision requires a communally oriented history, a lesson so well taught by colonial writers, as we discussed earlier. Hindutva ideologues, dreaming of Hindu Rashtra, have absorbed this lesson well and have invested in large-scale organized promotion of a particular version of history that supports the Hindutva ideology and their political project, and this is what we call 'WhatsApp history' and suchlike. The political imprint of this is obvious and insistent.

Historiography makes it apparent that historical reconstruction of the past has a wide context. Politics is part of that context. The political cannot be leached out of history or out of the historian, but it's important to remain conscious of its presence and not let it dictate historical reconstruction. All seasoned historians recognize this context and the influence it exerts on how the past is represented.

NAMIT: Yes. I think people forget that 'WhatsApp history' is just a facet of much larger and rising sociopolitical forces that academic historians could hardly have checked. It's part of a century-old project of religious nationalism, now more powerful than ever. While accessible and engaging histories by academics are always welcome—and there are many examples of it—Hindutva storytelling, with its gigantic and decentralized network, caters to a different need in contemporary India. Its simplistic, sensational and feel-good tales often start with declarations like, 'Historians will never tell you this!' Their fake claims about the Vedas are accompanied by fake certifications by the space agency NASA itself!

These stories artfully blend fiction and fact. They target legions of middle-class Hindus whose schooling has not equipped them intellectually to differentiate myth from history. Nor has later life done so. We've talked about how scientific and historical temper is awfully low even among our educated elites. My own extended family abounds in such people, who include engineers, doctors and MBAs. Barring a small minority, most are sitting ducks for organized disinformation, which again reveals our impoverished idea of education. The Hindutva ecosystem exploits their vulnerability through social media like WhatsApp. There's a saying, 'A lie or a conspiracy theory can travel halfway around the world while the truth is still putting on its shoes'—and ones that stoke undue fear of 'the Other' travel fastest of all.

Finally, ideologues now use AI to flood social media with historical content, such as 'artist's renderings' of historical societies and their artifacts and culture. These are often vivid and seductive, yet wholly implausible or fictitious. As such images and videos infuse into public consciousness, they will shape future Internet searches and further blur the line between fact and fiction. AI technology is making it easier to manufacture fake memories, pride and grievances. How will that play out?

In short, academic historians in India are up against massive structural challenges—such as a deeply flawed education system and organizations that have aggressively promoted chauvinistic storytelling about the past for decades—and are now doing so using the most advanced tools of mass communication humans have ever had. Believing that a lack of accessible historical writing by academics has caused this plague of disinformation is a fundamental misreading of the scale and nature of the problem.

Of course, accessible histories are absolutely essential too—not least to nurture the constituency of reason, critical thinking and good judgement in public life. We have many such books, but we need many more imaginatively conceived narrative histories, podcasts, lectures, documentaries and films that integrate credible scholarship with the big picture, especially in regional languages. That said, our problem seems to me much larger than the alleged shortage of accessible scholarship—it is structural and entangled with the sociopolitical realities of today's India. So while it's misguided to hold academic historians responsible for the rise of 'WhatsApp history', I also think they could do more to combat it in today's public realm.

ROMILA: A basic question we can ask is: why do the supporters of 'WhatsApp history' insist on a separate history, claiming that academic history is wrong and theirs is correct? If their history is based on reliable evidence and rationally determined causal connections, as history needs to be, then why are they so insecure in feeling the need to verbally and even physically assault academic historians and those that support secular, liberal ideas? Let's also be clear that such assaults routinely go beyond all bounds of social decency. What explains this appalling behaviour? It is inexcusable when they disallow persons with different views from theirs to give a lecture at a university. When history, written by trained, qualified and acknowledged historians is sought to be trashed by 'WhatsApp historians', then it is no longer a case of separate histories. It is a denial of history.

The Tantric goddess Bhairavi Devi, wearing skulls on her body, sits atop a decomposing corpse, and is accompanied by Shiva in the form of a devotee. By Payag (1630–35). Public domain.

12

Where Are We Today, Where Are We Going?

NAMIT: For my last question for this evening, it would be nice to step back and look at the big picture, at where our society is today. You know, one can reasonably argue that the situation is not *entirely* bleak—I mean, one can point to certain social indicators that have improved in recent times, but I still often feel distraught by our society's larger direction. Far-right culture and authoritarian politics is surging worldwide, including in India. And we've been discussing how a new idea of India based on toxic religious nationalism has taken hold. Neoliberal capitalism has idolized competition, and a garish idea of 'success' based on power, money and its loud display, all amid rising chronic unemployment. Rapid social changes in the last three to four decades, and rising class and wealth inequalities, have made people more insecure and vulnerable to status envy, populism and demagogues. Our big media has abandoned journalism and is now a vehicle of propaganda and polarization.

The autonomy of most of our democratic institutions, never great to begin with, has been sharply cut down. Communal ideologues employ powerful megaphones on the Internet, television and social media. For spewing hatred against minorities, they're rewarded by the ruling party! Disinformation is on steroids—in 2024, the World Economic Forum rated India the #1 country threatened by disinformation, aka fake news. We have an erosion of civil rights, more fear and less public trust. Public education is being starved of funds.

Consequently, most of our fellow citizens—a recent Pew Research Center's survey showed 85 per cent—now desire authoritarian rulers to set things right.[11] Large numbers have fallen for hateful ethno-nationalist beliefs that only raise social strife and suffering. Under such circumstances, how can concerned Indians foster scientific and historical temper in society? Or the fraternity, the sense of mutual care, shared meaning and forgiveness—all things vital to democracy? Instead, the market continues to penetrate deeper aspects of our lives in unprecedented ways, whose effects we only dimly understand. Add to this the coming ravages of climate change, ecological collapse and mass migrations, which will greatly amplify social stresses.

You've studied the evolution of India and of other human societies over the *longue durée*. What are your worries about India in the decades ahead?

ROMILA: We didn't have to consider climate change in the past.

NAMIT: That's true. Not this global kind. That's a googly for everyone! (laughs)

ROMILA: Some of the technology has contributed adversely to the growth of climate change. The greed for money assists these changes.

NAMIT: Exactly—especially technology that's deeply entwined with capitalism, which is propelled by a quasi-religious faith in endless economic growth through private profits. This model has been pushing up per capita incomes and ever-greater consumption of energy and materials for our mammoth, and still-rising, global population—a path that also seems to me fundamentally incompatible with ecological health.

And without ecological well-being, can there be human well-being? Sustainability has to mean something *real*! It can't remain a feel-good buzzword, as it so often is today. Living unsustainably will have its reckoning, and it's closer than we think. I believe future thinkers will devote far more attention to tracing how we developed the powerful blinders we still have on, which has led us to create this hyper-industrial civilization—one that is destroying the very life-support systems we depend on: clean air, water, soil, biodiversity and a stable climate. And we continue doing this while judging ourselves very smart!

But if you otherwise consider our social scene—pretend that this elephant in the room isn't there (laughs)—what are your worries about India over the coming decades?

ROMILA: My worries are really about India becoming unrecognizable.

NAMIT: In what way unrecognizable?

ROMILA: Well, you know, it used to be claimed that Indian culture was different from other world cultures because the people of India were concerned with values such as nonviolence and tolerance, and the ethics of a situation. It was almost automatic to invoke the words of Gautam Buddha and Ashok Maurya in this context. Yet today, few associate these values with India, if one looks at the media, public discourse, political speeches, or even what is taught in school.

Therefore, if you have a society in which ethical values are no longer even discussed, let alone practised, irrespective of whether they are the teachings of particular teachers or just significant social values, then you're in for a society that will not have democratic systems. Such a society will be ruled by mobs and demagogues, and it will be extremely difficult to maintain in it the values of a civilized society. And that's worrisome.

NAMIT: Yeah, I think the very damaged social fabric that's emerging will impede human flourishing in substantial ways. But despite this bleakness you see on the horizon, are there also some sources of optimism that you occasionally see?

ROMILA: I certainly can't see them at the moment.

NAMIT: What about with, say, the mass protest movements, like the one Indians had against the CAA (2019–20), or the big farmers' protest (2020–21)?

ROMILA: Those couldn't go as far as they should have because of the Covid-19 pandemic, could they? I sometimes wonder whether it's what appears to be the fading of a nation state—as it would seem is the condition India is approaching today—that leads me to worry about the kind of things some people say. For instance, that it is too large and too diverse. And that the salvation of this country will lie in its breaking into smaller fragments, where each fragment is more culturally cohesive. I would disagree. That may be an interesting theoretical argument but stops at that for me. I'm an old-fashioned nationalist. So for me, there is still that feeling that this subcontinent as it is, is a unity. Its administrative organization may have to be reconsidered. Some might argue that this unity was broken post-Pakistan and Bangladesh, and one would be deeply disturbed by further breaks. But I am sensitive to the various points of view of some who say that that seems to be the only way out and to others who suggest other future forms. That smaller units look after themselves much better, so forms of a sensitive federalism might be more suited. We have of course never had a subcontinental state in the past. But I would still underline a faith in the continuance of upholding the essential unity of the subcontinent.

NAMIT: That's very good food for thought. On that note, let's pause here for today, Prof. Thapar. Next time, I would love to dive into some of the more specific and contested debates, especially related to the period you know so well—ancient and early medieval India, but also beyond that. I can't wait!

A Pithora painting on cloth, Rathava tribe. Credit: Suyash Dwivedi, CC BY-SA 4.0.

13

On Migrations and the Lineages of Cultural Ideas

NAMIT: Prof. Thapar, let's talk about migrations and their downstream impacts. Over the last four millennia, several ethnic groups have entered and settled in the Indian subcontinent, with the Indo-Aryans perhaps the most consequential and transformative. Their imprint became the strongest in India's elite social groups. Recent studies in genetics, archaeology and linguistics have provided fresh insights into the cultural norms of their Indo-European ancestors, such as marriage, family, diet, lifestyle and religion.

We now understand that beginning in the mid-second millennium BCE, Indo-Aryan culture profoundly reshaped the genetic and cultural landscape of India. It saw its own Vedic religion evolve into Brahmanism, alongside forging and infusing the hierarchy of caste and an associated patriarchy into the social fabric. In northern India, it gave rise to multiple Indo-Aryan languages, or Prakrits, which drew their structural and grammatical foundations from Sanskrit. Today, all extant languages of north India are classified as Indo-European, sharing a common root with most languages of Europe—retaining only scattered traces of earlier subcontinental vernaculars in them, in bits of grammar, vocabulary, idioms, phonetics, gendered nouns and other residual features.

In comparison, the transformative impact of the incoming Turko-Persians appears relatively modest. Genetic science reinforces this view: while more than 15 per cent of the average Indian male lineage traces back to Indo-Aryan men, estimates by geneticists like Razib Khan suggest that less than 1 per cent derives from Turkic, Persian or Arab men.[12] The overwhelming majority of Indian Muslims descend from local ancestors who voluntarily converted to Islam, continuing a long tradition of religious shifts in the subcontinent, much like earlier shifts to varieties of Brahmanical Hinduism, Buddhism, Jainism, Tantrism, Sikhism, etc. That makes none of them any less Indian. Taken together, this suggests that the impact of Turko-Persian migrations was much less 'disruptive' to India's civilizational fabric than the earlier Indo-Aryan migrations.

However, today's elite groups, who identify with the Indo-Aryan substrate, often view the Turko-Persian substrate as the greatest misfortune to befall the land. Meanwhile, other groups, including many Ambedkarites and Dravidian nationalists, feel the same about the Indo-Aryan substrate!

Popular history is keenly interested in such debates, and I think academic scholars can offer a clearer understanding of which prominent cultural ideas are legacies of which groups—including local communities that long predated each newly migrant group—and which ideas got thoroughly mixed and were co-created. What do you think of such an exercise?

ROMILA: I think it's an exercise that certainly needs more work, because we have some rather warped ideas about migration and history, which we inherited from colonial historians, for whom migration was one agency of imposing a superior culture on inferior cultures. I would like to digress a little and say something about how we define culture in our times, which differs from the way it was defined in the nineteenth century.

This newer definition comes from usage in archaeology, history, social anthropology and religion.

The term 'culture', used for a historical society, is no longer confined to its earlier usage—meaning forms of self-expression reflected in philosophical thinking, a variety of literary forms, art and architecture. Such markers of high quality were often elevated to define a civilization. Efforts were made to extend these descriptions of a civilization's past 'high culture' into the present, even though every age generates its own cultures. In recent decades, however, the definition of culture has broadened. It now encompasses a wider collation of objects and practices—including customs, beliefs and knowledge—that together shape the pattern of life in a society. The study of these includes the interface between the many patterns of life across a region. The interface is essentially porous and malleable and is what keeps a culture alive. A society is therefore defined as having a pattern of culture, or even more than one culture if it is large and widespread. The pattern consists of various facets of living and thinking that are brought together in particular and characteristic ways.

Cultural patterns are not static. They have an element of the kaleidoscope. Some patterns change because they are carried by migrants. The latter either come in from elsewhere and there is a mixing and merging of patterns, or else they migrate from a home base and go out to settle among other cultures. The north-west of India both received and sent out migrants. The west coast from Gujarat to Kerala received Arab traders who were called Yavanas in Sanskrit sources—in continuity from the earlier reference to Greeks and those who came from the west—and who settled along the coast and founded new communities. The east coast did not receive migrants, but it sent out Indian traders, some of whom settled in small numbers in south-east Asia. The North-east received migrants from further east, and given this mixing, developed distinctive cultures.

In the nineteenth century, the history of migration was overshadowed by the obsession of defining the superior culture.

The debate on the coming of the Aryan speakers into India—the Indo-Aryans—was partly preceded by this obsession about which was the superior group. To this, we added some of our own pre-colonial prejudices about superior and inferior people and the hierarchy of castes.

We're now moving away from this obsession with superiority and inferiority and are beginning to treat migration as the interface between two cultures: the host culture and the guest culture. It is seen as cultures that come literally face to face, and how they relate to each other. Obviously, when this happens, unless there's a predominance of power in the hands of one, the interface is usually an exchange of different aspects of culture at various levels, the size and impact of the exchange being varied. We really do have to look at the various migrations again and see what they brought and what resulted.

For example, most scholars today agree that the speakers of Indo-Aryan originated outside the boundaries of British India, arriving from Central Asia. The earliest philological studies stated that there was a group of Aryan speakers in north-eastern Iran and another in north-western India. Indo-Aryan used in north-western India was a cognate of Iranian-Aryan used in north-eastern Iran. It was a close relationship. King Darius of Persia, in a 490 BCE inscription written in Iranian-Aryan, declares that he is an Arya, and the language is presumably the identifier. This is something people often overlook. These were two groups of people each speaking a language of the Aryan category. They were using related languages and worshipping some of the same gods and practicing similar rituals. If the Vedic Indo-Aryans were performing the Soma ritual, the Iranian-Aryans were performing what they called the Homa ritual, the 's' sound being replaced by the 'h' sound from one language to the other. Hence the river Sindhu (Indus) in Indo-Aryan becomes Hindu/Hind(h)u in Iranian-Aryan, and the Iranians refer to the people who live beyond the Sindhu as Hindus, which is a geographic and not a religious descriptor. The use of 'Hindu' to describe a set of religious beliefs emerged only in later medieval times.

It might be worth doing detailed comparative studies of the differences and similarities between these two guest cultures and how they evolved. What impact did the host cultures have? For instance, linguistics tells us that elements of Dravidian entered the Indo-Aryan language from around mid-second millennium BCE, which is a clue to the kind of interface that may have happened between the Aryan and the Dravidian speakers. Elements of Dravidian are missing in Iranian-Aryan, which implies that in Iran they were not in touch with Dravidian speakers. Such clues indicate the kind of cultural impact of migration and the regions where it happened. It also tells us what the language of the host culture might have been. One doesn't then go on to say that the Indo-Aryans were superior to the Dravidians, or that they were superior to whoever existed in Iran. The nature of the contact between the Indo-Aryans and the Dravidian speakers in northern India has to be examined, to ascertain if there was any change in both societies. That's the more important question. The Rig Veda refers to an unusual category of people that are called the *dasi-putra* (literally, 'slave woman's son') Brahmins. For a Brahmin to be a dasi-putra, raises a problem. What was their identity and how did they come to be called the way they were?

What I'm suggesting is that the reality of guest–host relationship in this period has not yet been adequately investigated by historians and linguists; research in this area is still in its infancy. Such an investigation is necessary, for it may reveal—as some of us suspect—that there was no singular overwhelming Aryan culture. Instead, there might have been extensive exchanges and mutual influences, with the resulting cultures across the subcontinent shaped not only by the Indo-Aryan but also the pre-existing host cultures. The details of this are now being debated among scholars. Unlike earlier times when there was little evidence of extensive activity in the peninsula, recent excavations have revealed a variety of Megalithic and other cultures that seem not to conform to the north Indian patterns.

NAMIT: Yeah, I think it'd be useful to have a clearer sense of what cultural traits of a migrant group later became prominent, what local groups contributed, what new things they created together and so on. You spoke about languages. I'm also thinking of other cultural traits. Take the Yamnaya people who were in the Pontic Steppe from around 3500 BCE. Scholars believe they were among the first speakers of a proto-Indo-European language from which descends Vedic Sanskrit, and over 400 languages now spoken as a first language by almost half of humanity. One of the many easterly descendants of the Yamnaya were the Sintashta people (c. 2200–1800 BCE), who were the direct ancestors of the Indo-Aryans. The Sintashta rode horses and chariots and had a culture of raiding. They also performed horse sacrifices. According to archaeologist David W. Anthony, 'The funeral sacrifices at Sintashta settlements showed startling parallels with the sacrificial funeral rituals of the Rig Veda.'[13]

In addition, the ancestors of the Yamnaya had evolved lactase persistence (the ability to digest milk in adulthood; the Harappans likely didn't have it). Cow milk became an important source of protein and gave them nutritional advantages, which might explain why they accorded a special status to the milk-giving cow (but not to the water buffalo because they didn't have any in central Asia). Lactase persistence appears in multiple descendants of the Yamnaya, including the Indo-Aryans. And like pastoralists across the world, these groups also ate the meat of the animals in their herds, including cows after they stopped giving milk.

Further, many Indo-European groups, including the Indo-Aryans, had a three-tier social division that later evolved into the four-tier varna system in India. Genetic science suggests that they also had a patriarchal culture, where women left their natal families to be with their husband's family. Many of these groups, including the Indo-Iranians, later came up with the custom of sati. Even a wife of Philip of Macedon, father of Alexander the Great, died as a sati because her Thracian people, also of Yamnaya descent, had this custom. And several descendants of the Yamnaya, including the Indo-Aryans, ritually sacrificed horses.[14] Clearly, all this is not a random coincidence but a legacy of common origins.[15]

So what I'm saying is that the host society in India ended up with a lot of these cultural traits from the Indo-Aryans. It'd be good if we were able to more clearly identify the lineages of such ideas—that custom X has come down from group Y, that certain other ideas have mixed or unknown or unknowable origins. That's where many of our culture wars are today, and I think that's where the historian can weigh in with more informed perspectives.

ROMILA: Also the historian can demonstrate and argue for looking at more factors and features that went into the relationship between host and guest than we have conceded so far.

NAMIT: Yes. A recent book that was very interesting to me was Peggy Mohan's *Wanderers, Kings, Merchants*. She talks about the evolution of Indian languages and how they were likely shaped by the mixing of various groups and other societal changes.

For example, genetic studies show that the Indo-Aryan migrations were male dominated. After they move in, they need women. And it's not like local women are just lying around waiting for them. The two in fact represent very different cultures—different languages, religions, lifestyles, etc. The Indo-Aryans are pastoralists of lighter skin, and in the subcontinent's north-west, they mostly run into agriculturalists with darker skin.

Add to this the suggestion from genetics that men in the male-dominated Indo-Aryan migrations mainly reproduced with local women, likely by displacing many local men, perhaps through coercion and violence. Indo-Aryans famously had horses and chariots, you know. They were no meek refugees; they became the dominant social class in their adopted home. Their disproportionate genetic impact, evident in north Indian populations today, suggests an asymmetric power that helped them propagate their genes faster.

Howsoever it happens, we get these combinations of Indo-Aryan men with women who speak proto-Dravidian or other vernacular tongues. Their offspring have lighter skin colour than their mothers and are influenced by both cultures. In this patriarchal subculture, the male child learns Vedic Sanskrit and various hymns and chants, except they're now inflected with words, idioms, and accents from his mother tongue. Vedic Sanskrit gains retroflex sounds that are unique to the languages of the subcontinent. This suggests a possible social reality that shaped the evolution of Indo-Aryan languages.

ROMILA: I would like to emphasize that the point is not that one holds this as a theory but one holds it as a possible opening to looking at cultures differently. It has to find reliable evidence to support it, and it has not been fully investigated in these terms. But it is a hypothesis. That's really all that people like me are suggesting. In this interface of cultures and languages, people inevitably need an opening for communication, and this is really what we should be looking for.

A Santhal painting by Chandi Hasda. Source: Lalit Kala Akademy.

14

History Speaks of the 'Visible People'

NAMIT: Prof. Thapar, it seems to me that much of early India's social history is based on records left by the 'visible people'—those who created texts, monuments and other durable artifacts. These groups were mainly urbanites and settled farmers and they spoke Indo-Aryan languages like Sanskrit and Prakrits, as well as some non-Aryan languages in the peninsula. They practiced the big religions, whether Brahmanic or Shramanic. Yet they were a numerical minority before the Common Era and likely remained so through the first millennium CE.

Meanwhile, the 'invisible' majority of India consisted of forest dwellers, nomadic pastoralists, hill tribes, swidden cultivators, outcast groups and others who may have interacted with the visible people but mostly from the margins. Their culture was often vastly different, featuring different gods and customs. It was often more egalitarian and matrilineal, and they spoke mostly non-Indo-Aryan languages.

So my question is: Is it not unfair to regard the culture of a minority as representative of early Indians? Popular history now does this routinely, but could this be because most historians of early India, perhaps unintentionally, have encouraged it? Why don't historians frequently remind us that they are primarily speaking of a culturally dominant minority while also raising the visibility of the rest of our ancestors?

ROMILA: Since we do not have a count of the population from those times, we have to assume that the impression we have of majorities and minorities is correct. I would tend to agree broadly with your assessment.

Well, I think there are various reasons for the questions you raise. One is of course that the way history was constructed in the eighteenth and nineteenth centuries was one where the dominant superior group spoke Indo-Aryan languages and that's continued and hasn't been especially questioned. Additionally, this minority initially had a strong oral tradition that included ritual texts and rituals employed in part to support their dominance. Added to that, what needs attention in this construction is that the focus is on a minority which is a dominant cultural entity largely to the exclusion almost of what else was going on at the same time. This suggestion needs examination. In part this is because there is no written evidence from the non-Indo-Aryan speakers. Nor is there an oral tradition going back to earlier times that has been definitively located so far. Therefore the evidence may come from archaeology, and we need to do much more excavation of cultures contemporary with the Indo-Aryan of northern India.

An interesting thing happening at the moment is that archaeological evidence is surfacing, dating to the second millennium BCE, in a number of post-Harappan sites in the northwest, in Haryana and other parts. Was this from where there was a move, slowly and gradually towards the Ganges plain? The question that we used to ask when we were students was: what about the rest of the country, what was happening? We didn't know.

Now interestingly, archaeology is providing clues about that. For example, peninsular India in the second millennium BCE hosted many Megalithic sites. And the Megalithic culture, long dismissed as a subsidiary culture, has now to be seen as much more forceful. This could lead to a substantial change in the balance between what was happening in the north with the spread of Indo-Aryan Vedic culture and what was happening in the peninsula with the spread of the Megalithic cultures. The Megaliths are not like the Harappan finds; they represent a distinctly different culture. If there can be more archaeology in the peninsula and south India, we would have a fuller picture of what has been found in both the north and the peninsula. For instance, archaeology has thrown up new questions from the spread of Megalithic sites in the Vaigai and Kaveri valleys and nearby areas, with the possible urban centre at Keeladi. For a slightly later period, there is the important site of Pattanam.

NAMIT: Yes, sites such as Keeladi, Adichanallur, Pattanam and Sivagalai point that way, even as scholars debate what the finds mean for urban culture and its timelines. Something big is emerging. It seems India's second urbanization—after the Harappans—happened both in south India and in the Gangetic plains simultaneously, starting in the sixth century BCE. This will significantly rewrite that era's history. It'll likely become another nail in the coffin of that silly-yet-persistent idea that Indian civilization begins with the Vedas.

ROMILA: The question inevitably is: what was going on in the circumference, in the periphery? What was going on, and can this be related to the literary sources? We have to consider the difference in the sources too. Literary sources are quite unlike archaeological sources. The kinds of information one will get, the kinds of arguments that will be made, will differ between the two.

NAMIT: Yes. I'm also quite interested in communities that didn't leave significant traces because, typically, state societies do that. State societies have greater productive capacities and tend to leave behind the more durable artifacts and big monuments . . .

ROMILA: But state society comes about in the middle of the first millennium BCE.

NAMIT: Right, I am saying even then, even when state societies come up and we have the Mahajanapadas (the sixteen kingdoms and limited republics) and then the Mauryas, there are plenty of other groups all around who are still perhaps the majority of the population, who don't leave durable records or artefacts. I mean with many early forest-tribal groups, we have little more than bits of pottery or ornaments of shell, bone, clay or stone. And I've often wondered if scholars are looking more closely at the indirect evidence of their culture. For example, in what genetic science says about their social norms, in the goods they traded, or in the dominant culture's appropriation of their gods, ideas and customs—a starting point for exploring the beliefs of non-state peoples who likely had those deities. Alongside, and a bit later in the first millennium CE, we have Tantrism and its many forms that rise from the grassroots. These non-Indo-Aryan expressions of culture are radically different. So it's disappointing that there is little emphasis on studying these subcultures, especially by Indian scholars. One example I recently came across is R.C. Dhere's work, which shows how today's Lord Vitthal evolved from a regional hero-figure venerated by shepherd communities into a Vaishnava deity embraced by a large cross-section of society in Western India, including Brahmins.[16] Incidentally, no Indian saw it fit to translate his 1984 book from Marathi to English until a white American did so in 2011. This is symptomatic, and it raises awkward questions. Nor do we have any latter-day Indian counterparts to the anthropologist Verrier Elwin. That said, interest in studying folk and tribal cultures is on the rise among Indian scholars—though who knows when these perspectives will find the space they deserve in mainstream history textbooks.

Historians can also incorporate more anthropological studies from the last two centuries, particularly of adivasi groups, who still have oral traditions. Theories based on anthropology or ethnographic analogy can be tested against archaeological data. While we still can't be sure about the continuities of contemporary beliefs and practices with much earlier cultures, these studies can nevertheless be indicative and suggestive of the many ways our ancestors saw the universe, the natural world and the meaning of life. Their origin stories and cultural archetypes are different from those of the dominant culture. Their ideas and fables and legends are incredibly diverse and distinct from today's dominant cultures, and they've existed all along in our land—and still do. Some recent scholarship, for instance, in archaeology by Shereen Ratnagar, in sociology by Abhay Xaxa, in colonial ethnography by Sangeeta Dasgupta, and in linguistic and cultural anthropology by G.N. Devy, have raised interest in adivasi cultures and their trajectories of change but much more work is needed.

The number of adivasis is comparable to the combined population of Britian and France. Despite the homogenizing forces of modernity and Hinduization, they speak over 300 distinct languages and inhabit diverse, nature-centric world views, which some of them call *Sarna*. Most had systems of collective rights to land and resources, rather than private property. They've had their own histories of change, adaptation, discovery, innovation, and lately, loss and dispossession. But the modern we, who see ourselves as progress-bound, civilized and possessors of the truth—even as we hurtle down a path that's destroying our ecology, destabilizing our climate and causing a mass extinction of species—we largely see them as static and primitive, as people who have nothing to offer the rest of society, and who would be better off if only they awakened to the glories of industrial development, wage labour, private property and consumerism. Our history textbooks mostly ignore them. That part of our history and culture is just not emphasized enough.

ROMILA: There will not be enough of that until we overcome the obsession that Indian history and culture in early times were dominated by a single Indo-Aryan culture, followed by a series of what were also viewed as superior cultures, which contributed to creating a civilization. The concept of civilization the world over is confined to the culture of the elite. We rarely search for an interface, for instance, between adivasi culture and that of the royalty that hunted in adivasi backyards. Yet, when aspects of adivasi culture are investigated, such as religious beliefs and forms of worship, the interface clearly hovers. I am fascinated, for example, by the way in which ideas of deities and rituals are taken from the dominant Hindu representation and rendered in adivasi idioms, as in their paintings.

We have to view the location of other cultures in relation to each other. We also have to consider that some aspects of Indo-Aryan culture may have evolved from a mixed culture. Most cultures cannot be described as unalloyed with any other. It was an evolving culture that showed local strands as well as assimilation and contributions from others.

NAMIT: It's interesting you say that. Because early Vedic religion, or Vedism, was apparently very ritualistic and incantatory. It lacked concepts such as maya, karma, dharma or moksha, which we associate with Brahmanism. These later ideas were part of what turned Vedism into Brahmanism in the first millennium BCE. They may well have been inspired by the host culture's beliefs, including even the idea of meditation that multiple Harappan artefacts suggest—with people sitting in meditating postures.

ROMILA: This has been suggested, but as of now remains debatable.

NAMIT: That may be debatable—especially the claim that Harappan artefacts show a meditating proto-Shiva—but many such things, it's also clear, were taken from the host culture, that what we call Brahmanism is built upon the incoming Indo-Aryan cultural substrate but also incorporates a range of local borrowings and adaptations.

ROMILA: Talking about mixed cultures, can I come back to my pet obsession, the *dasi-putra brahmana*? Why is this qualifier used? If the category of Brahmins is receiving recruits who were not Indo-Aryan speaking, these latter may well have contributed a few facets of their religion and language that were then incorporated into Indo-Aryan rituals. What is very interesting I think, and not enough attention has been given to it, is that Hinduism is said to have its roots in Vedic culture and that's why the Indo-Aryans are very important, etc. If you look at the history of Hinduism from century to century, some fundamental beliefs of Vedic culture such as the belief in deities, are opposed by the Shramanic religions such as Buddhism and Jainism. The latter are called nastikas (non-believers) in Brahmanical texts. This points to dissenting views and these continued into later times. This can lead to the question as to whether this dissent drew on possible pre-Vedic belief systems.

Then in the first millennium CE, there comes to the surface what some of us call the Puranic religion—that is, the central worship of Shiva, Vishnu and the later Shakta cult, and various other deities, which get established. It is assumed that the Puranic religion, especially Shaivism and Vaishnavism, are Indo-Aryan. This raises interesting questions. The earlier Vedic deities Mitra and Varuna become less important and later, Indra and to some degree Agni, also. Meanwhile, the centrality of Shiva and Vishnu grows enormously. How much did the Puranic religion reflect facets of the Vedic religion? How much of it resulted from the amalgam that had been taking place through the cultural interactions between communities. Vishnu and Shiva were not dominant gods in the Vedic tradition. The rituals change, the big yajnas they used to have and some of the large-scale open-air altars, and the sacrificing of animals and all the rest of it now comes down to smaller-scale pujas and rituals. The sacrificial altars give way to temples, which become sacred locations.

This is a different concept of the sacred space and location, which may have come from the Buddhist *chaitya* (hall of worship), but we don't know that for sure, and most important, icons are introduced and rituals of worship are developed around the icons. This procedure didn't find mention in the Vedas. Where did the idea of temples and icons come from, and how did they relate to the more extensive rituals of the Vedic religion? They are familiar to the Shramanic religions, which the Brahmins have referred to as prevailing among the nastikas.

A certain history and continuity become associated with Hinduism, but there is also the articulation of a different turn to the religion more in matters of ritual than of belief but having some influence on belief. Because such phases of new forms are characteristic of Hinduism but are absent—at least to the same degree—in the Abrahamic religions, they are seen as distinctive facets of the history of Hinduism. These make it a richly diverse and complex religion. We have to ask how similar the Vedic religion was to the Puranic religion. When discussing facets of Hinduism, there is some hesitation to point out differences except among scholars, since the practitioners of the religion would prefer to see it as a continuity. But we see that the texts are different, the rituals are different, the places of worship and the forms of worship are not identical, as also some of the actual values and religious forms that are adopted. Some continue, but some don't. So one really has to do a meticulous comparative study of the different historical phases in the evolution of Hinduism. The phases bring to it the larger numbers and the richness of the variations.

NAMIT: That's really interesting! What about the dominant thoughts and ideas in the Upanishadic corpus? In your view, how much of that comes from the Indo-Aryans versus from non-Aryan cultures? How would you analyse the Upanishads in terms of their cultural influences?

ROMILA: I think it's mixed, and we have to ask whether it represents a single strand of thought or a few strands woven in. Some questioning arose in the teachings of the Buddhists and the Jains. We should inquire whether this in any way gave a different dimension to the philosophical arguments that were drawn from the Vedas. Some have argued that the Buddha and Mahavira questioned the Vedic religion, and that the questioning provided a different perspective. What this can imply is that there was an imprint of Indo-Aryan thought, but it did not annul the presence of elements of other religious thinking.

NAMIT: Do we know where ideas such Brahman, Atman and Moksha come from?

ROMILA: I wouldn't really know—I am no expert on that. But I imagine that anyone, whether a group or an individual, who meditates and thinks about questions like who am I, what is this world, how do I relate to it, will come up with some answers. They may not be the same of course, but they do share some similarities across the teachings of different religions.

NAMIT: I find it interesting that early Buddhism seems to have incorporated more elements from the local substrate. It appears to have more non-Aryan influences in it. Here, I find it interesting that Buddhism arose on the eastern fringes of the Indo-Aryan zone (or Aryavarta), and a lot of the early Buddhist art also reflects much older spiritual ideas and traditions. So it seems like it has a lot more grassroots fusion going on.

ROMILA: It may have more fusion in themes. But we have to remember that the actual representation—the icon of the Buddha—surfaces in various geographical locations of northern India, in the north-west and the middle Ganga Plain, from Gandhara and Madhya Pradesh and then continues south down to Andhra, and then to Sri Lanka. The regional imprint on the style and aesthetic is clear. It's not as if it started in one place and the same style of the image spread uniformly. What interests me is the imprint of regional identities that were evident in the art.

NAMIT: Iconic representations are one thing, and they do have regional flavours, but I am referring more to the civic and philosophical aspects of Buddhism. In the teachings of the Buddha and institutions such as the Sangha, Buddhism appears socially more egalitarian, which is not quite an Indo-Aryan ethic. Divinities such as Sri and yakshis and others associated with fertility and harvest find a more prominent place in early Buddhist art, along with lay women. Female body adornments—bangles, jewellery, hip belts, etc.—remind one of the Harappan aesthetic. This comes through in the Sanchi Stupa and clay figurines from the Mauryan era. Above all, early Buddhist art emerges from a substrate culture that seems more female-friendly.

ROMILA: It may suggest that. We need to pay closer attention to the objects—both utilitarian and artistic—used by societies that have so far remained on the margins of historical reconstructions. Also consider the *Therigatha*, a Buddhist text that records the songs of the Theris. Nothing quite like it exists in Brahmanical Hinduism, perhaps for the obvious reason that there are no orders of nuns in early Hinduism, nor therefore the social concessions that go with such institutions. I find that to be a noticeable difference between the two traditions, although in Puranic Hinduism the independent role of the woman is registered in the icons of Durga and some other goddesses.

NAMIT: Another Buddhist text from early India that I think has no equivalent in Brahmanical Hinduism of the time is *The Lion's Roar*, a significant Mahayana text by a Buddhist woman called Srimala, a teacher and philosopher who lived in south India in the Ikshvaku kingdom of the third century CE. Srimala affirmed that women were no less capable than men of being teachers and thinkers, and she advanced the idea of female Buddhas—articulating, in effect, the principle of the universal potential for Buddhahood.

*Six-armed Durga Mata and Tiger [*bagh*]* by Ramrati Bai Baiga (2021); Ganesh by Nannusingh, Jaipur. Courtesy: The Crites Collection.

15

Patriarchy and Gender Relations in Early India

NAMIT: That leads nicely to my next question—about looking at Indian history through a gendered lens. I wonder if we can explore how patriarchy and gender relations have shaped the lives of Indian women. As in much of the world, patriarchy in India likely became systemic with the rise of early state societies. In contrast to many hunter-gatherer societies, which were often more egalitarian and matrilineal, the emergence of pastoralism, settled farming and organized states created conditions for men to accumulate more power and wealth. In parallel, the spread of the Indo-Aryan patriarchal culture began to displace older, more matrilineal traditions that had existed in parts of the subcontinent.

That said, the outcomes haven't been uniform. Across India's vast landscape, different regions, communities and social classes have afforded women varying degrees of autonomy and equality. Could you speak about this historical variation? How do you assess the lives of women in the subcontinent from the perspective of gender equity? And which cultural traditions, in your view, have fared better—or worse—in this regard?

ROMILA: It is difficult to generalize about gender forms and relations over a span of two millennia or more. There are two aspects that I think one must underline as a historian. One is the variation in the degree of prevalence of either patriarchal or matrilineal norms in different types of societies. Looking at archaeological cultures, hunter-gatherers appear to have been more matrilineal. The assumption is that the men hunted whilst the women gathered food and looked after the children, though some have questioned this neat division of gender roles, or its universality, across groups—arguing that some women also hunted, some men gathered and so on. Would there be much change with pastoralism where the basic resource was the herd in the care of the herdsmen? Cultivation probably did bring about a change with a permanent settlement on land, cultivated by both men and women but where the produce was probably stored and controlled by men.

With the rise of new vocations such as trade and exchange, men often assumed a larger role, since these activities sometimes required travelling to distant places. As a result, urban centres tend to reflect patriarchal social structures. This outline is not meant to be taken rigidly but simply to suggest that a diversity of social forms is to be expected—and that the structure of a society can significantly shape the roles and status of different genders.

Historically, one has to consider how social forms shaped gender forms. It has been argued that the Harappan society may have been matrilineal, at least in its early stages and then it may have gradually moved in the direction of patriarchy and patriliny. This theory is based on the finds of the Mother Goddess figurines and the depiction of scenes on vases and seals involving female figures. But such depiction can refer to many other concepts and not necessarily indicate matriliny. One could also argue that the body language of the male sculptures suggests a certain male superiority, and therefore it was a patriarchal society. As we know from later periods of Indian history, many firmly patriarchal societies were also worshipping Mother Goddesses. One has to therefore look for more definitive evidence of the one or the other. Societies across the subcontinent will inevitably be mixed. The study of their rituals from this perspective is a good source of clues, as are their social activities. Changes in society affecting gender are most frequently thought of as those when the male takes charge, and this may begin with controlling the family and more particularly the women—mothers and sisters—and may evolve into a more definitive control.

Nearly a century ago, when historian A.S. Altekar wrote what was then regarded as a foundational text on the history of women in early India—though it is no longer seen that way—he treated women as part of a single, virtually uniform category, with little room for differentiation. This framework produced sweeping generalizations about women in Indian history. Much has changed since then. Scholars now recognize a wide range of women's roles and activities across social and economic strata, thanks both to more analytical readings of old texts and to the discovery of new sources and fresh lines of inquiry.

For instance, the anthropologist Iravati Karve wrote with great sensitivity about the women depicted in the Mahabharata and on how various women had varying ways of coming to terms with the problems they had to face. Her book *Yuganta: The End of an Epoch* makes fascinating reading. There were other sources with different messages such as the inscriptions of Prabhavati Gupta, who ruled as the Queen Regent in the fifth century after her husband died and until her son came of age. Her inscriptions suggest that she was a powerful ruler. But we have to explain why this was possible at that time and place but was not common elsewhere in the country. In another category, we have women Bhakti *saints* who shaped regional Bhakti movements, such as Andal in south India, Mirabai in Rajasthan and Lal Ded in Kashmir. Taken together, this information points to the many social levels at which women were prominent, and this information can also be explored to explain why this was possible in these particular societies, as also to understand the problems that these women had in establishing their kind of religious expression.

These different levels are reflected in the references to women generally. Women marrying into royal families or into those of wealthy landowners, drew their status in most cases from that of their husbands. Some intervened in the activities of their husbands, such as their activities in politics, but most stayed away. Their daily lives were different from those who married into Brahmin families. Among families of traders, the social levels differed from the wealthy traders to those of lesser incomes who were shopkeepers and suchlike. Successful courtesans were well off but at the lowest level were the prostitutes, who had a meagre income and were under the vigilance of government officers and their income was taxed. In the rural areas, the women worked with their husbands in the fields. There is little reference to women in a supervisory capacity. When women speak of the reason for their joining a nunnery, it is partly to get away from household chores. In many ways, therefore, the lives of women have to be viewed from diverse perspectives. To study this, one has to observe and explore more than just the two categories of patriarchy and matrilineal societies. Yet, these two were in themselves distinct.

Patriarchy was strong in the Indo-Aryan culture. The Dharmashastras permitted upper-caste women hardly any freedom, as they were to be controlled by their father, husband and son, in the three phases of their life as daughter, wife and widowed mother. The rare woman philosopher such as Gargi, who is often quoted to prove the high status of women in early India, is actually the proverbial swallow that does not make a summer. The Shramana sects, including Buddhists and Jains, were a little more liberal in the freedom they allowed women, and their texts present a picture of women being active in social life. That women could choose the alternate life and become nuns was also at one level a form of freedom although they did have to conform to the rules that determined the activities of a Buddhist or Jain nun. The more the Indo-Aryan culture is venerated through historical time, and the greater the emphasis that it is given today, the more it implies the entrenching of patriarchy.

But again, one of the things that puzzles me is that Indian society, in the first millennium CE going into the second millennium, is strongly patriarchal, yet it is also the point at which there is the popular worship at all levels of society of the Mother Goddess. Is this something that needs an explanation?

NAMIT: I have a take on that. We know that during the first millennium, Tantric and other folk religious traditions featured a host of powerful goddesses. Over time, however, as these deities get incorporated into the expanding Brahmanical pantheon, their roles change, their power changes. Take the example of Pampa, the river goddess from the Hampi region. She is a powerful and independent deity, while her husband, Virupaksha, is lesser known, a sidekick god. But once the two are presented as forms of Shiva and Parvati, their power reverses. Pampa turns into a mere 'consort' of Virupaksha, who later even becomes the state deity of Vijayanagar. The grand Virupaksha Temple gateway depicts Pampa as sitting on Virupaksha's lap, like a child! And as Brahmanism and patriarchy spread, this happens over and over to lots of deities in the subcontinent and goddesses keep losing power.

So you end up with a situation where these goddesses stick around but something has fundamentally changed, mirroring the changes in society. The goddesses continue to be worshipped, perhaps out of cultural habit, even though, with a few exceptions like Durga and Kali, they are now the sidekicks of the more powerful male gods.

ROMILA: That makes sense in terms of what one observes. My problem with it is that every time I have been to live with a community in the rural areas, and I have had brief stays with a range of them, as for example when excavating or just doing fieldwork, they are all worshipping mother goddesses, and they are all praying avidly to women goddesses, although they don't neglect the male deities. Yes, there is obviously a ritual that is connected with Shiva, Vishnu and some other male gods, but in effect, the immediacy of worship and the immediacy of communicating with a deity—I have the impression, and I may be wrong—I have the impression that beyond the metropolitan centres, there is more communication with the female deity than with the male. The male is more ritualistic. You know what you are supposed to do and the kinds of offerings to make. But your more desperate prayers, from your inner being, seem to me somehow more tied up with female deities. I may well be wrong. I have not inquired into or studied this question. It could even be a variation that derives from caste or status. This would have to be investigated. I think it would make for a worthwhile investigation.

NAMIT: That's a fair point. One does see that, even as it varies across groups and regions, a bit more in eastern India for instance. Urban upper-caste groups seem to have less of this culture than subaltern groups and adivasis and other rural communities. It seems to me loosely a function of how remote a group is from the dominant Brahmanical culture.

ROMILA: As we discussed earlier, one of our enduring problems is that non-upper-caste cultures are only sparsely represented—and often entirely absent—in modern historical writing. We just don't know what to do. We either don't have the sources or we don't want to use the sources or we don't want to ask the kinds of questions that require asking. There has been almost a kind of negation of histories other than those of the elite. History has been the elite history of the upper and the established castes. We really have not been too concerned with the rest. The rest are there, almost as part of the background. Whereas, in fact, the subtlety of that interrelationship I think is something we haven't grasped. It is now beginning to change among professional historians who understand that one cannot generalize about society if one quotes the concerns of only one section of it. Fortunately, new interest has emerged in these areas, partly led by scholarship focused on women and Dalits.

NAMIT: That's well said, and from what I observe too, this change has picked up pace among professional historians, particularly those based in academic institutions that have prioritized social and intellectual diversity in their hiring practices.

Let me return to the issue of patriarchy. We see goddesses continue to hold a prominent place across India, but there's a striking disconnect: despite this widespread veneration of female deities, the actual status of women in Indian society has remained deeply unequal—both today and historically. How do you make sense of this paradox?

ROMILA: I think one could put it provocatively and say that there is a contradiction in Indian society, where the public manifestation of religion is male dominated, but the quieter relationship with godliness has a closeness to the feminine in it. How does one come to terms with this? In the performance of public functions, is there a concession that they are basically patriarchal, or perhaps have slowly changed from matriliny to patriarchy? In other arenas too, we may ask whether the day-to-day expression in religious emotion or rituals of prayer are also patriarchal or is there much more of the feminine in them?

NAMIT: But is that a contradiction? Under any patriarchy, one would find spaces where women can exercise some autonomy of thought and action. All patriarchies tend to permit some such spaces to women while also diminishing their humanity vis-à-vis men by denying them educational and professional opportunities, limiting their sexual autonomy, barring them from public positions of power, normalizing violence against them, saddling them with unpaid and unrecognized domestic labour and so on.

ROMILA: One would have to look then at the expression of dissent, especially among women, which may not be obvious but which is quietly recognized. I don't know if this makes the point, but devadasis attached to temples go through the ritual of singing and dancing in public, which is not entirely, but it may, to some degree, be a defiance of patriarchy. Yet, the association is ostensibly with worshipping the deity.

NAMIT: True, dissent among women has surely existed all along—even though it may not be recognized as such, or may not be too visible in historical texts, whose production was pretty much controlled by men.

I want to pick up on another point you made, this emphasis on the Mother Goddesses, especially in rural India and among adivasis. This phenomenon predates the Indo-Aryans. The Harappans had a plethora of female figurines in clay, some of which may have been Mother Goddesses. Is it possible that we have a long cultural continuity here?

ROMILA: It may well go back to earlier societies. Creation is dependent on birth; it is that which ensures continuity, without which the world cannot exist. Birth cannot happen without a woman—unless one is speaking in the language of mythology. The worship of a female figure with some attributes could be the logical origin of society and worship. My point is that we may have many studies of female deities and Mother Goddesses, but have we as historians correlated these with the kinds of societies we have had in the past—or perhaps even in the present? It's an important issue in any society and also ties up with the questions we raise about origins, and the explanations we give for the condition of various categories of women in past society.

NAMIT: Speaking of origins, we've already considered that certain patriarchal norms and ideas appear to have come down to us from Indo-Aryan culture in early India. Recent genetic studies of burial sites in Central Asia show that centuries before the Indo-Aryan migrations into India, among many early Indo-European groups, women were married away from their natal family—only they, and not men, were expected to relocate to the spouse's family. Anthropologists, such as Sarah Blaffer Hrdy, associate patrilocal residence, as this norm is called, with patriarchy (hunter-gatherer societies tend to be more flexible and gender-egalitarian). In the early Indo-Aryan tradition, women already play second fiddle and are barred from leading fire rituals, which becomes another reason for them to prefer male offspring.

In our great epics, especially the Ramayana, gender disparities are notable. For instance, Sita's life is dictated almost entirely by the decisions of men, and her worth is judged above all by her chastity—a virtue elevated not for her own sake, but to safeguard male honour. Then there is the custom of sati, first reported in the Mauryan era and which also appears in the Mahabharata. But it is seemingly an older idea that also appeared in Eastern Europe, West Asia and Iran, where other early Indo-European speakers lived. I've already mentioned the example of the Thracian wife of Philip II of Macedon (Alexander's father), who ritually self-immolated on her husband's funeral pyre. This custom seems rare in ancient India but later expanded in some regions and elite circles, even as it vanished elsewhere in the world. Common or not, the mere presence of sati as an ideal reveals something about how the Brahmanical elites imagined women and their role in society, suggesting an oppressive kind of gender power relations. It was also of course opposed by many local groups of non-Indo-Aryan origin, such as the Tantrics, who embodied diverse grassroots systems of belief.

As caste-based patriarchy and control of property intensified over time, so too did the obsession with purity and the policing of women's sexuality—not the least to secure uncontested lineage. In the Brahmanical tradition that's codified in the Dharmashastras, women are far too often imagined as property, pliant domestic labourers and vessels for reproduction. They are not regarded as responsible, rational beings capable of independent thought and will. Instead, they are often depicted as impulsive seductresses, bearers of an unruly sexuality, who need to be tamed and married off as children to avoid trouble. Thereafter, women are expected to remain economically and socially dependent on the male head of the household—the *ghapati*—serving as obedient wives, mothers and caretakers under his authority. Indian women scholars have explored all this.

So yes, we see this superstructure of patriarchy among the elites. But both within and certainly beyond it, alternative roles and degrees of autonomy were also afforded to certain kinds of women—such as those from aristocratic backgrounds, as you noted earlier, whose power derived primarily from their association with their husbands. Another example is of women in the Buddhist Sangha who could 'pursue philosophy', as Megasthenes noted, though their status was unequal to that of men. The courtesans and the devadasis exercised certain forms of agency and influence. There was also some acceptance of gender and sexuality diversity, what we now call the LGBTQ+ spectrum. The Tantric tradition—emerging from its non-Indo-Aryan roots and rising from below to penetrate even elite cultures—was substantially more egalitarian for women. You also noted some examples of women Bhakti saints, such as Andal and Akka Mahadevi, who, deriving strength from their devotion to a personal God, pushed back against patriarchal norms in their lives. So there are all these different types of experiences that women have also had, as you suggested minutes ago, but which we often forget.

ROMILA: I did a talk some years ago, the main thrust of which was that women's histories have been written in the early days, when women were taken as a large uniform block of society and treated as a single unit, as I mentioned. Distinctions of status, caste or class or gender were few. The prevailing belief was that women were revered during the Vedic Age. The ideal woman was commonly portrayed as a *pativrata*—one devoted to her husband and adhering to the norms prescribed in the Dharmashastras. There was minimal effort to explore what women themselves were experiencing, expressing or the actual conditions of their lives. The same generalization was applied to all women, whether they were elite women or whether they were working women, whether they were from the north, south or the east. The region makes a difference since there were diverse rules about rites of passage for women—identification by birth, exogamy and endogamy in marriage, rules of inheriting property, death rites. The pattern of culture would dictate the rules, and these differed in different regions and in varying occupations and statuses.

The view of all women constituting a single unit broke down when feminist historians started writing and women were seen as part of differing social groups—as were the men—and their status in the hierarchy derived from the historical context. What I was trying to say in the lecture was that the society of women is also stratified, as is that of men. It is also stratified by various considerations. It cannot be studied as a single large uniform unit. One cannot generalize about 'women' as a whole and then apply the generalization to a specific case. One must be specific about which category of women one is speaking of, just as one is specific about men. Scholars like Sharmila Rege went further in pointing out the blind spots in mainstream feminist discourse towards the concerns of Dalit women.

Once one starts doing that, one finds, first of all, that patterns of patriarchy, matriarchy/matriliny, may not be as strongly bonded and confrontational as we thought. There is some adjustment, except when it comes to marriage. There are also some concerns which relate to both patriarchal and matrilineal society, and the one influences the other depending on the circumstances. Social historians and social anthropologists should perhaps be investigating these aspects of the relationships together, since there will be texts that mention social history and may need some explaining.

One would also like to know how the rules were determined. The elite groups of the Vedic period are generally described as patriarchal. But was society continuously as strongly patriarchal or matrilineal as some imagine, or were there degrees, more and less, of each? Did castes differ on this? It would seem that marriages among ruling families that involved different religions did not observe customary marriage rules, else the assessments and gradations would have become very complicated. When the Mughal ruler married into a Rajput ruling family, were there questions asked by either the Rajput or the Mughal relatives about which marriage rules were being observed and which were perhaps being broken? Or was it accepted as essentially a political statement?

NAMIT: Yes, but the thing is, the fact remains that today there are hardly any matrilineal societies left—a sliver in Kerala, a pocket in the North-east, a few tribes in central India. They were once a lot more common but have simply lost out to patriarchy, perhaps after passing through stages where degrees of both existed, as you note. I suppose this shift owes much to that classic dynamic of subordinate groups imitating the norms of a dominant colonizing culture at the expense of their own. That is also partly how Christian colonizers, who went on to rule various parts of the world, gutted local matrilineal systems, in Africa, Indonesia and elsewhere (often also through coercive laws). And it seems to me that in much of India too, the juggernaut of the dominant colonizing Indo-Aryan culture being what it was—strongly patriarchal—these matrilineal societies withered away, following similar patterns.

ROMILA: One would have to do a careful analysis of the kind of patriarchy or matriliny that is prevalent in different societies, and what are the degrees of freedom or control in these as applied to the different social categories. Is it the same all the way down the social scale? The women who belong to the royal families, are they as much under the thumb of patriarchy as the women cultivating fields? There would be a difference in the social hierarchy as practised, although the texts—such as the Dharmashastras may suggest uniformity within the rules as given.

NAMIT: There would've been differences, yes, some better, some worse in each group. The Dharmashastras, focused on elite groups, may have created the illusion of uniformity. But even among the elites, I suspect there was more diversity in real life.

ROMILA: I think that kind of analysis needs to be given more exposure where it already exists, and there should be more discussion of the differences and why they are observed. It will have to be done where it doesn't exist. It seems to me that women of the lower classes, who laboured to produce food or other goods with direct economic returns, were relatively freer than most women of the higher classes, until the mores of the upper castes eventually reached down and their freedom was incrementally curtailed.

NAMIT: Yeah, it has been said that upper-caste women had it worse in many respects, since they faced more stringent rules of caste purity, which demanded tighter control over their sexuality. I like historian Uma Chakravarti's description of Brahmanical patriarchy as a dual system of domination in which gender and caste are deeply intertwined. She has argued that the control and subordination of women are the means through which both caste purity and hierarchical order are upheld.

Among upper castes, for instance, girls were frequently married off in childhood—before they could make a sexual 'mistake' that might render them 'impure' or 'damaged goods'. Widow remarriage was also largely prohibited—a restriction that was rare among lower-caste or adivasi communities. Widowers of the upper castes could of course remarry freely, but widow remarriage risked complicating matters of inheritance and lineage (*gotra*). There was also the economic incentive to retain the widow's unpaid labour, services and the dowry she brought. One way to ensure all that? Declare the widow inauspicious—and even blame her bad karma for her husband's death. How sweet Brahmanical patriarchy is!

Even in royal families, things were not necessarily better, right? At best we could call it a mixed picture, with regional variations. Some queens, such as Rudrama Devi, Nur Jahan and Sembiyan Mahadevi, became movers and shakers and occasionally even monarchs, but they were the exceptions—rising despite the system, not because of it. South India appears to have been relatively better for women, as it seems even today. But even in the south, women were scarce in mid-tier administrative and political leadership roles in state hierarchies. In some medieval states—such as Vijayanagar, the Rajput kingdoms and the Mughal empire—royal women enjoyed some luxuries and could cultivate certain artistic talents. But they were typically confined inside walled palaces and gardens, guarded by eunuchs, not to be seen by male strangers, and allowed out only in covered palanquins. So we have that too.

And royal families long ago began trading women as part of the wheeling-dealing among men—to cement borders or to advance their territorial ambitions, etc. They were mostly pawns in the games of royal men. This wasn't just in India. The ancient Greeks did that too. Incidentally, the Greeks too had an Indo-European lineage descending from the Yamnaya. They also frequently saw women as property. I recall the legend about Seleucus Nicator giving away his daughter as part of a deal with Chandragupta Maurya.

ROMILA: We do see that in royal families, where intermarriage is more often led by political strategy than by caste or religion. The Mughals and Rajputs, for example, do intermarry and some of the most prominent Mughal figures are born of these alliances. But the point is, women are treated as property. Women are the means through which alliances are made and all the rest of it. That said, these women are also playing a public political role, although not too visibly. Sometimes of course they are really visible, but most of the time, these women operated within—and were constrained by—a deeply patriarchal system. Which raises an important question: Were there any women who refused these roles altogether? Who said, 'I won't do it?'

NAMIT: Perhaps, but how many of them had the choice?

ROMILA: They may not have the choice, but what is also of much interest is that Mughal royal writing has both the memoirs of the emperors, and also of several women, such as Gulbadan Begum, Jahanara Begum and others. Reading them critically might reveal whether they accepted patriarchy and its nuances, or how they felt about being under its rules.

NAMIT: I haven't read them, but I wouldn't be surprised to find that they did resist patriarchy, in overt and covert ways, despite the indoctrination, incentives and threats to play by its rules. I think that all subordination provokes at least some resistance, whose expression would then vary based on a woman's circumstances and her personality.

ROMILA: We also have stories of women bhakta saints, such as Akka Mahadevi and Meerabai, that reflect their objections to patriarchy. Very often they bypass traditional gender roles and norms and make their own way in society.

NAMIT: Right. And then there is the phenomenon of courtesans, which is a whole different thing.

ROMILA: Yes, the courtesans, and the devadasis. The extent to which they were subjected to patriarchy needs to be assessed further.

NAMIT: When it comes to courtesans, or *ganikas,* we often hear of a few who became famous and fabulously wealthy. Trained in the fine arts and aesthetic refinements, some of these women lived in upscale parts of town and sometimes inspired literary figures, such as Vasantasena in Shudraka's *Mrcchakatika* (*The Little Clay Cart*). Unlike most upper-caste women, they escaped being treated like 'property' owned by men. They held a measure of power, social esteem and autonomy, at least until the late first millennium CE.

But it's also true that their success depended on their ability to appeal to the dominant male gaze and elite male society. They had to have certain types of talents and attributes that appealed to elite men, and only such women could rise to the top. Their status remained conditional and precarious. Many more faced exploitative sex work and servitude. So they were all very much embedded in a patriarchal culture.

ROMILA: The rules were certainly made by the men. How the women used their earnings would be another question of interest. There is a contradiction between having to obey the rules in order to be appreciated and to get the earnings and having the right to do what you like with the earnings should you want to use them in a way not approved of by the patrons. What are they spending on and to whom are they making donations? How much hold does patriarchy have on them when they consider such questions? By the way, the *Arthashastra* also has a section on sex workers whose earnings are taxed by the State.

NAMIT: Right. It seems that female prostitution as a legal and taxable profession has been a recurring feature of Indian civilization. Its presence is also attested by the *Kama Sutra* and by foreign observers such as Megasthenes, Alberuni, Razzaq, Barbosa and others. Many states apparently had laws to punish those who harmed sex workers.

As for devadasis, they were attached to specific temples, serving as dancers and musicians. They pioneered the dance form Sadir Attam, a precursor to Bharatanatyam. Some devadasis commanded great respect as artists and performers and received gifts of land or jewellery. Domingo Paes spoke well about their status in the city of Vijayanagar in the early sixteenth century. But there was often a darker side to this, right? Customs varied but in large parts of India, devadasis, usually recruited young, were also expected to grant sexual favours to the temple's priests and patrons, and I wonder about the quality of their lives. I often think that the freedom and autonomy of devadasis, as a group, have been much exaggerated by later thinkers keen to minimize the pathologies of this institution.

ROMILA: It could have changed from early to later times. But here again we cannot treat them as one group. Their earnings and status would vary according to their social level. Kumkum Roy, for instance, has explored the lives of devadasis and courtesans in *The Power of Gender and the Gender of Power* (2010), and how things changed over time, along with numerous other aspects of women's lives in early India.

NAMIT: I also like that book by Kumkum Roy. She has tackled a lot with great finesse.

Finally, what about the issue of women and property rights in early India? Today, we regard it as central to gender equality and women's autonomy. On the one hand, many inscriptions reveal queens and other wealthy women donating to Buddhist monasteries and temples. Celebrity courtesans, who were single, often grew wealthy and donated property. The daughters of devadasis had equal rights of inheritance as the sons. There was also the provision of *stridhan*—a married woman's wealth that was solely hers—accrued through voluntary gifts. Matrilineal systems were of course much better for women on the issue of property rights. For the rest, we hear that daughters were not entitled to equal patrimony, that widows inherited nothing of their dead husbands' wealth and so on. No doubt the situation again varied by social class, caste and region.

How would you characterize women's ownership and inheritance rights and legal control over landed and other property versus men in early and medieval India?

ROMILA: It would be helpful if we knew the nuances and variations in the income of courtesans and devadasis. Knowledge about women's rights to property of various categories would tell us much about the rights of women generally, or at least those who were entitled to hold property, a number which I suspect must have been small. But again, there would be some variation from situation to situation. Women of royal families were patrons and donors and obviously had access to some wealth, although probably under the control of the appropriate male member of the family. Courtesans, or at least the more successful ones, did have property of which they were the sole owners and which they could dispose of as they pleased. Buddhist sources mention a well-established courtesan, Ambapali, who gifted a park to the Buddhist Sangha.

It's important to note that such women who made grants represent a tiny minority. Data on the lives of most women in early India—those who were active partners in small households—is not plentiful, but there is some in Buddhist texts and this has been studied. There are also references to another group: the *dasi*s, whose lives were far from enviable. These enslaved women worked in households and were treated as property, often included as items in gifts. For instance, the *dana-stuti* hymns in the Rig Veda ('hymns in praise of donations') as well as references in the Mahabharata, where Yudhisthira gambles away his wealth, mention a number of dasis as part of that wealth. Dasis were indispensable to every moderately affluent household, yet they had no rights or autonomy. Their status was low, their labour hard and their wages minimal. They were expected to submit to all—whether male or female. So this too was part of the reality of some women's lives in early India.

'Bandhavgarh forest on fire' by Santoshi Bai Baiga (2022), Baiga Adivasi tribe in eastern MP. Courtesy: The Crites Collection.

16

Nonviolence and Tolerance in Early India

NAMIT: Let's now talk about how early Indian culture is often described as relatively nonviolent and tolerant. To what extent was this true? I mean, people often cite Buddhism's and Jainism's advocacy of nonviolence, which even extended to animals. This is significant. But ideals are one thing, reality another. As Walter Benjamin said, 'There is no document of civilization which is not at the same time a document of barbarism.' A fundamental attribute of every state society is organized violence. States enforce class hierarchies, property rights and taxation through violence—or threats thereof. State societies typically grow through war, and they aggressively expand urban and agrarian spaces at the expense of forest dwellers, pastoralists or other marginalized groups and natural ecosystems. While some might see early India's religious syncretism as relatively tolerant—and I'll come to that in a minute—its caste system had intolerance and violence baked in, as did its patriarchy.

By 'violence', I mean not just physical violence but also systemic psychological violence and abuse which is often no less debilitating to a person's well-being than physical harm. The threat of violence can be pretty awful too. My definition also includes violence to non-human species, the ecology and fragile ecosystems.

So I have two related questions: (1) How do you assess early India's record on nonviolence and tolerance in the social realm, and (2) What is the record of early India's dominant social groups on ecological stewardship of the kind we historically associate with adivasis and indigenous peoples worldwide? This question may seem odd, but I'm raising it because there is a trend among certain Hindutva ideologues who superficially speak of decolonization while pushing Hindutva as the path to achieving it (rolls eyes)! Their narrative asserts that Hindu Sanatan Dharma—touted as an 'eternal way of life', despite the historical implausibility of anything being eternal—once embodied sound ecological stewardship, which they claim was disrupted only with the arrival of European colonizers. Because it suits their purpose, they cleverly ignore the wide gulf in ecological sensibilities between the expansionist Brahmanical elites and the adivasis, who are now classified as Hindus by the Indian Constitution but who were historically very distinct.

So yeah, first, how do you see India's record of nonviolence and tolerance in the social realm?

ROMILA: The record of nonviolence and tolerance in early India is similar to that of most other societies. There really isn't anything especially different. It may have gone up or down over time. There were, however, the Shramana teachers—largely Buddhist and Jain—who preached the centrality of *ahimsa* (nonviolence) and *karuna* (compassion) as taught by the Buddha and some others. That is notable. Contrast the Buddha's views on violence and how it is to be avoided as far as possible with the Hindu tradition, where it is sometimes discussed as contingent violence. If there is a really nasty situation, then violence is allowed but by and large, it is preferable not to be violent. Some have argued that this form of contingent violence is present in the teaching of the Bhagavad Gita. I have often thought that if the Buddha had been Arjuna's charioteer on the battlefield of Kurukshetra, there would surely have been a different discussion on violence and nonviolence. There is a difference between rejecting violence, irrespective of the circumstances, and allowing it to be contingent in a situation that may require it. However, this could be a debatable point.

In Hindu and Buddhist literature, violence is not altogether discarded or banished, but one could say that whereas Hinduism accommodates it to some extent, Buddhism in the same situation would tend to disallow it if possible. The presence of violence is challenging to an ethic that disapproves of it, hence the tendency for nonviolence not to be absolutely insisted upon. Buddhist teaching may be more sensitive to the presence of nonviolence.

The examples of violence are plentiful. There is the violence related to survival—of hunter-gatherers, of cultivators when clearing land and the animals on it, of traders in their caravans who would kill animals that threatened them. But then there's all the *unnecessary* violence, driven by greed and expansionary pursuits. The burning of forests and consequent killing of animal life, including hunting for fun, is referred to. A consequence of agricultural expansion was conflict between sedentary farmers and mobile pastoralists whose ranges were threatened. The much-applauded conquests of conquerors—and I am not just talking about foreign conquerors but also those within the subcontinent—were examples of large-scale violence. All the little Indian kingdoms that were at war with each other, they were indulging in intolerance and violence.

Major statements on this come from the edicts of Ashoka. Why would an emperor call for tolerance among the different sects, if tolerance was already in place and there was no violence? Obviously, there was a problem, so he had to ask for peace to set it right. In the early edicts he does not refer to violence ensuing from wars. That comes later. In the thirteenth Rock Edict, where he confesses to being contrite at having caused so much suffering because of the Kalinga War waged by him, the ethic of ahimsa and tolerance that deeply moved him, seems to have come from his sense of the value of human life. Significantly, he does not quote from any text when addressing the public. There are many conquests, of later rulers such as Samudragupta, or Harsha, and the constant wars between the many dynasties, which were not lacking in violence, and this was happening all the time. Most of the rulers, including the well-known rulers in the subcontinent, spent much time in battles and consequent violence.

The image of the great king is of one who is a conqueror, and conquest assumes violence and intolerance. So I really don't buy the theory that early Indians were especially nonviolent or tolerant.

NAMIT: That's a very good point. Why do we instinctively regard conquerors and ruthless empire builders as great? Rather than see them as antiheroes, we adore aggressive power, military triumphs and expansionary pursuits in kings, especially if they're now seen as belonging to 'our people'. We equate domination of others with civilizational strength and well-being. We also tend to value the 'high culture' that empires often encourage through courtly patronage while ignoring their awful costs and downsides: their ethos of coercive extraction and concentration of wealth, their organized exploitation of nature and people, etc. I'm not singling out Indians here; it's a global malady. I think this lopsided way of looking at things now infects too many of our assessments in the modern world too.

Returning to violence in early India, Upinder Singh offers a similar view to yours in her book, *Political Violence in Ancient India*. It's also interesting to me that like the *Iliad*, the Mahabharata too is suffused with violence and slaughter, though it powerfully laments its consequences in the Stri Parva. And speaking of state violence, another aspect of it comes to mind—punishments meted out by medieval Indian states, some documented by foreign travellers, as in Vijayanagar. It seems no worse than the violence of medieval European states, but it was still utterly awful: torture, dismembering, beheadings, elephants goaded into tearing men apart, thrusting wooden stakes through the belly and so on. Horrid stuff!

But what do you make of the argument that because of a certain syncretic streak in early India's big religions—and Indians not obsessing over some divine writ in a book and so on—they were relatively more flexible and tolerant in the religious dimension? At the same time, they made life much harder for people in the social hierarchy dimension. Every caste had to know its place and rules of engagement with other castes; else, it would be punished with violence and/or social boycotts. So-called honour killings still continue. This overlapped with violence that was baked into Indian feudalism, including bonded labour, land seizures, and collective and individual punishments such as flogging and mutilation. Then there is the long history of gender violence, as in dowry murders, various kinds of abuse, etc.

So it seems to me that Indian culture has doled out its violence and intolerance in some similar but also in many dissimilar ways than cultures elsewhere. Its forms and their distribution were different across social and familial spheres. I suppose such differences are part of what it means to be a different culture.

ROMILA: I think there is that difference, yes, and there are contradictions. For instance, if sati is taken as a religious ritual, does its implicit violence define religion? And yet, at the same time, the same religion can also endorse meditation as almost a form of ritual, which is entirely non-violent and tolerant. The same religion can be preaching non-violence yet have major rituals that are violent, say if animals are sacrificed. So how do the two become part of the same religious belief?

NAMIT: Yes, I think such contradictions exist in all religions. In medieval times, many relatively pacifist strains of the Bhakti Movement coexist with periodic incidents of violence against people over cow slaughter, or even the mere suspicion of it. Such lynchings continue to this day—largely against Muslims and Dalits—and that's an example of religious violence. Untouchability, too, is suffused with violence, both physical and psychological, and it has long enjoyed the impunity of religious sanction. All these contradictions certainly exist within Hinduism though they're different from those in Abrahamic and other religions.

ROMILA: Right, I think one problem I have is with how the Hindu religion has been defined. There has been a lack of clarity on the part of both colonial scholars seeking to understand it and by some subsequent Indian and other scholars who tried to fit it into the framework of the Abrahamic religions. I mean, when we started talking about religion in modern studies, we tended to go by what the colonial scholars were saying, and in the nineteenth century, many of our histories of Hinduism were based on texts either interpreted or influenced by colonial thinking, and some Indian reactions to it. Colonial thinking seemed to argue that from some perspectives, this religion was different from Islam and Christianity. But their problem was that they understood religion as that which followed the pattern of the Abrahamic. Therefore, how was this religion to be made to fit the structure of the Abrahamic religions?

Hinduism was not based on the teaching of a particular individual, which then requires his rules of discipline, his explanations that become a catechism, his teachings collated into a book and a strict conformity to rituals, which then spreads as a religion. This was not the pattern of Hinduism. There were teachers, and sacred books, and rules of religious observances, but these were circumscribed and represented not by a single uniform structure but by a range of sects. Each of these had their degree of independence even if they identified themselves as broadly related.

Interestingly, this appears to have been a partial aspect of virtually all religions in India, even the Abrahamic. The latter did have sects wherever in the world they were established, but the role of sects vis-à-vis the religion was perhaps not quite the same as in India. Before broad-based inclusive religions became the norm in modern times, religious identity among Hindus was more often that of the sect. The identity of being 'Hindu' is not so frequent in earlier times. For example, as recently as two generations ago in the Punjab, people seem to prefer to describe themselves as Sanatanis, followers of Sanatan Dharma, or Arya Samajis, members of the Arya Samaj and others like Radhaswamis and so on. Hinduism as a religion was more frequently expressed through the sects, which were fundamental to the organization of the religion. But when the term 'Hindu' began to be used in public discourse, then this association became more regular.

But where Hinduism does overlap with Abrahamic religions is in the organization of its institutions. The parallel to churches, mosques and monasteries were the temples and monastic institutions, such as *ashrama*s *and matha*s. Such institutions help spread and discipline the religion and also receive patronage and donations. The historian therefore studies these as socio-religious institutions since their function is not solely religious and they do have an impact on civil society. Interestingly, from the above perspective, Buddhism and Jainism in their social formations are more similar to aspects of the Abrahamic religions, although their initial denial of deity makes them different in terms of their religious message. Textual evidence from early sources suggests that the Buddhist *chaitya* (hall of worship), *stupa* (relic mound) and *vihara* (monastery) were earlier institutional patterns created before the arrival of the Abrahamic religions in India.

What this difference suggests is that in Hinduism, people can adapt their religious practices to changing needs—drawing from their own tradition and taking elements from others—to form new sects. If such a sect gains acceptance, it becomes part of the broader religious landscape; if not, it remains a minor tradition that may persist or eventually fade away. If one studies Hinduism by asking who founded the sect, what were its teachings, what was its history, did it join other sects or remain distinct and why, and so on, one gets a rather different idea of its development—one that contrasts with the trajectories of other major world religions. This highlights a different kind of social organization that demands as much attention as the rituals associated with it.

This kind of structure was not uniform across the subcontinent, but it had a strong presence. In a sense, this is demonstrated in what is referred to as the Bhakti Movement, which originated in the late first millennium in south India. Through the second millennium CE, it was manifested in variant forms in different regions of the subcontinent. It is almost suggestive of coinciding with the rise of regional identities. What is more striking is that it did not require the entire population of the region to live according to the rules of the dominant sects. In fact, the majority of people appear to have practised a rather freer religion, which offered a choice of the deity for primary worship, the form of worship, the prayer and sometimes even aspects of belief. One could worship in a temple or a *dargah* or a *gurdwara*, and still be respected as a good Hindu.

Let me clarify this to avoid misunderstanding: I am not suggesting that Hinduism—or any other religion—was inherently superior to others. My point is simply that Hinduism had a distinct structure that set it apart from other major religions. It is this structure that we should be investigating. In fact, many of the questions currently being raised about it still require deeper inquiry and analysis. For instance, how were non-Hindu communities converted to this religion? Is it possible to argue that in India religions evolved differently from the way they did in other parts of the world? Islam in India was different because most Muslims were not confined solely to the formal beliefs of Sunnis and Shias. The majority practised rites and rituals of which some were Islamic, some were non-Islamic, some were whatever they were. The Sufis made a different kind of contribution. I think what one means by 'religion' has to be redefined given that it shows various interesting dimensions when looked at historically. There were contradictions from dissenting groups, of which there were many, as well as accommodation by groups that accepted what was taught. We need to look more closely at variant philosophies which suggest that this is a different story from that of Europe, or of West and East Asia, and this different story has to be investigated in a different way.

The modernization of Hinduism over the past two centuries gave rise to new forms, notably through the many nineteenth-century *samaj*s, such as the Arya Samaj, the Brahmo Samaj, the Prarthana Samaj, the Ramakrishna Mission and others. These movements were shaped in part by the emerging needs of a new middle class and were influenced by the frameworks of Abrahamic religions. The twentieth century, however, marked a significant shift with the rise of Hindutva—the ideology of Hindu religious nationalism. Unlike earlier reformist currents, Hindutva became a vehicle for religious mobilization with explicitly political aims. That's why I refer to Hindutva as 'Syndicated Hinduism'—it represents a sharp departure from pre-modern Hinduism. Its attempt to imitate the structure of Abrahamic religions likely stems from viewing those traditions as global and institutionally powerful.

But Hinduism's long-standing diversity—its tradition of divergent sects and localized practices—belongs to a very different phenomenon. I am not a specialist in the history of religion, but I do think that there has been a conceptual slippage in understanding how these variant forms have functioned historically within the Indian religious landscape.

NAMIT: Yes, what came to be called Hinduism has long been an evolving, dynamic and distributed conglomeration of sects and faiths, big and small—not centralized or unified in any way. To a historian, there is nothing that is 'sanatan', or eternal, about it.

The evolution and structures of Abrahamic religions differ indeed. I think Hindutva is partially a product of Abrahamic religion-envy and the politics of nationalism. Like you, I also see Hindutva as a major departure from historical Hinduism.

More a blight, if you ask me, akin to Zionism and Islamism—all colonial-era developments, too.

Let me then return to my earlier question. Could we say that, when it comes to violence in our ancient and early medieval past, there was less violence between *religious* groups but no less of the other types of violence: social, military, etc.? Could we say that religious groups indulged in less violence against each other in early India?

ROMILA: I don't think so because these sects could be quite antagonistic if they chose to. There was a possibility of friendly relations but also the possibility of hostility with violence. Small groups working out their relationships and their rank in the social hierarchy using religion, can be a very complex exercise. Ashoka speaks of Brahmins and Shramanas as two distinct categories, each with its own meaning. The grammarian Patanjali, in the *Mahabhashya*, compares their relationship to that of a mongoose and a snake. For me, this is a very telling statement. This tension continues over time: the *Rajatarangini* refers to the Brahmins' ill-treatment of Buddhists, while inscriptions from South India record Shaivite hostility toward Jains. These were not cordial or peaceful relationships; they were often marked by conflict and violence.

NAMIT: Yes, violence was certainly a factor in the decline of Buddhism in India. The Chinese pilgrims mention some of it, but other Buddhist and non-Buddhist texts speak of it too. Many Buddhist monuments were destroyed by Brahmanical groups—not just in India. *The Mahavamsa*, the great Sri Lankan Buddhist chronicle, has some gory details on the Cholas' treatment of Buddhists in Sri Lanka in the tenth–eleventh centuries.

To your example of Shaivite violence against Jains in Tamil Nadu, one can add examples of Lingayat violence against Jains in Karnataka and of periodic violence between Shaivites and Vaishnavites. While researching my documentary film on the Maha Kumbh Mela of 2013, I learnt that even within the Shaivite fold, the centuries-old *akharas*—such as Juna, Avahan, Niranjani, Atal and other akharas of ascetic monks trained in basic martial arts—have often resorted to violence and even fought pitched battles. Deep down, their conflicts are over social and political dominance, only ostensibly triggered by questions such as who will take the first dip in the holy Ganga on the auspicious *shahi snan* days of the Mela!

Now, about my second question. How do you see the historical record of early India's dominant social groups on ecological stewardship? Were they any more responsible than their counterparts in other parts of the world?

ROMILA: I don't think so. I mean, ecological stewardship depends on the information you have about the world you are living in and what you observe, the physicality and the functioning of it, and so on. And I think the information of the Indian elite was similar to that of elites elsewhere. It was different in some ways, they didn't see the world in identical ways, but informationally, Indians were not markedly ecologically aware or environmentally concerned. However, they did seem to have been more knowledgeable about the therapeutic value of plants, or else one can say that this knowledge has survived into modern times to a larger extent than in many other places.

It was a society aware of the environment and appreciative of the plants and trees in the midst of which it lived. Going to live in the forest was often a metaphor for exile but also for living a life that was believed to be in conformity with nature. The Ramayana is full of the beauties and benefits of life in the forest. Of the four stages of a man's life, the ashramas, the fourth and last was ideally spent in exile in the forest or the wilderness. It is another matter that probably few people undertook this fourth stage since there are so few references to such persons. The population was far smaller, leaving vast tracts of land relatively untouched by human activity. The pressure on the environment was far less, and forests seemed like another world altogether. Nevertheless, forests were also burnt—often brutally so, as in the destruction of the Khandava-vana in the Mahabharata to clear space for Indraprastha, so it was a practice likely familiar to the epic's authors and their audience. Or the forests were cut down when land was granted for cultivation and ownership to those that the king wished to reward. Still, such interventions were limited in scale, constrained by the modest size of the population.

NAMIT: Many people point at Hindu mythologies and say, look, there are so many animals and plants and nature deities in it, so we obviously had this special place for nature. But I've often thought that this mythology by itself is not enough for ecological stewardship. For that, people must also feel in their bones their dependency on nature, that they too are a part of nature. They need to be intimately aware of its rhythms and vulnerabilities, and to then use resources from their environment in sustainable ways—to not take from it more than it can regenerate, to not pollute it more than it can absorb and so on.

That's a whole different kind of knowledge system, closer to that of many adivasis historically, or of many indigenous people elsewhere. Elite and urban groups, raised in state societies, invariably lose this knowledge that's really quite vital for ecological stewardship. They grow apart from nature and start aspiring to 'control nature' for their benefit at larger scales. In fact, their unequal wealth partly derives from ecological violence and theft of land and forest resources from marginal groups who live differently. Meanwhile, as their milieu changes, their ancestral myths mutate or get repurposed to serve other ends. We see this sort of process unfolding across the world, including India. Is that a fair assessment?

ROMILA: I think that would be fair, yes. Also, when one talks about relationships to nature, for example, there's a tendency for people to say, oh yes, medicine, we were brilliant in terms of understanding cures, natural cures, what plants and animal parts can be used for, and so on. But I'm not sure that we knew much more than in any other part of the world. Our plants were different, so the cures varied. Perhaps even our ailments were not identical, although some must have been the same. They just saw it differently; we see it differently. I think that every society looks at the world it's surrounded by and says, what am I to do with this, and works out an interrelationship between these different aspects of the world around it. We saw it as much as anybody else did, such as the Chinese, and the Europeans. We may have used our information differently and that would be understandable since our environments differed.

NAMIT: My final thought on violence and intolerance in our past is to agree that, yes, on the whole, Indians in real life appear to have been no less violent or intolerant than others, though they doled out their violence and intolerance differently than other cultures. But I still feel Indians were distinctive in the sense that they reflected a great deal on the problem of violence and tolerance, turning these into ethical and moral concerns. Some figures who did so, at least in their later lives, include the Buddha, Mahavira, Ashoka, Harsha, Akbar and Gandhi. This is something special and distinctive, don't you think?

ROMILA: We have to differentiate between the space that was taken by expositions and discussions of these values in our texts versus those of other civilizations. These values might have been discussed more often in our texts, but they do not seem to have dramatically curtailed intolerance and violence in society. There might be a small difference and more discussion in ours but perhaps not enough to describe Indian civilization as strikingly different on this score. The major exponents of ahimsa and karuna were the *sanyasi*s, *sant*s, *shramana*s, *pir*s and suchlike. These were people who had distanced themselves from society in various ways. They were what I have called the 'opters-out'. Nevertheless, these holy men—whether genuine or fraudulent—were and are respected by members of Indian society as were their traditions granting them the liberty of dissent. Akbar, for instance, invited them to his court and had conversations with them. Gandhi's *satyagraha* is a partial concession to their thinking.

One could argue that a strand of Indian philosophy did engage with questions of tolerance and nonviolence—but interestingly, this was more often found in the writings of those whom Brahmanical thinkers labelled nastikas, or non-believers. It is striking that Ashoka's edicts drew little attention from later Indian rulers, nor did they spark much discussion in classical texts on ethics. While Buddhist texts at least acknowledge him, Brahmanical texts remain notably silent. At best, we might say that although Ashoka himself is not mentioned, the ethical issues he raised were taken up by some philosophers and debated within the broader landscape of philosophical discourse.

The other more historical, or rather historiographical, aspect we must keep in mind is that this theory of Indian civilization being more given to ahimsa and karuna is an idea that took shape and gained strength as an aspect of Indian nationalism. All nationalisms seek features that distinguish their own nations from others. In the Indian case, this resort to nonviolence and tolerance was projected as an Indian claim to being somewhat superior compared to the others. The claim was never seriously analysed and gradually it came to be accepted that to question it would almost amount to being anti-national and anti-Indian!

NAMIT: Well, by those yardsticks, some would consider us both anti-national and anti-Indian (nervous laugh).

Idital painting of the Lanjia Saora tribe, made using rice powder on a background of red oxide. Idital paintings are partly made to symbolize collective devotion to the tribal deity 'Idital'. There are sixty-two types of idital paintings, each for a specific occasion or ritual (Odisha State Tribal Museum). Photo: Namit Arora.

17

The Emergence of a Common Indian Identity

NAMIT: Let me move on to the matter of Indian identity. Over the centuries, many foreign travellers passed through India: Megasthenes, the Chinese monks, Alberuni and others. These travellers noticed a cultural distinctiveness about the subcontinent, and called its inhabitants Hindus—then a non-religious term for all peoples east of the Sindhu River in al-Hind. They saw them as different from people elsewhere in the world, though their perceptions were seemingly based on their interactions with the dominant and literate groups, or the 'visible people' of the time.

But did Indians themselves broadly share any sense of a common identity, whether religious or secular, in early or medieval India? Did they see themselves in any sense as 'us here' versus 'them outsiders', roughly aligned with subcontinental boundaries? If not, when did the first semblance of such a common identity emerge across India, at least among a significant subset of its people?

ROMILA: If you speak in subcontinental terms, I would say very late. Megasthenes doesn't mention the similarity all the way across. He refers to different groups, different practices,

are they leaving the others out? That's a very deliberate cutting off. There are no clear boundaries. Does Aryavarta extend from the northern mountains to the Vindhyas? It is said to be between the two oceans, so is it between Sindh and Bengal, or between Kerala and Tamil Nadu? That's not clearly defined, it's vague. It's the same with Bharatavarsha and Jambudvipa. The geography is neither clear, nor consistent.

It seems to me that a sense of unity within the subcontinent begins perhaps with the European colonial conquest. Maybe a little earlier? The Marathas, for example, are all over the place—in the Punjab, UP, Bengal, Tamil Nadu, though briefly in some places. But are they seeing all this as one land and one people? I don't think so. I think they are seeing it as conquering different kingdoms and cultures, not as anything consolidated. But I really don't know enough about eighteenth-century history to be able to answer that question. I think that the sense of Indianness pervading the subcontinent, as a uniformly recognizable identity, is a colonial-era development.

NAMIT: I think so too. Prior to that, in early and medieval India, identities were largely fragmented—shaped by region, language, kinship, religious sect, tribe, varna, jati, or combinations of these and more. However, a few scholars, such as Shonaleeka Kaul and Aloka Parasher Sen, hold that there *was* a shared civilizational identity in this period. They point to Sanskrit texts whose authors seem conscious of cultural commonalities across the subcontinent, as well as to certain shared customs and the popularity of epic stories.

I remain unconvinced by such reasoning. To begin with, these same Sanskrit texts, as B.D. Chattopadhyaya argues in *The Concept of Bharatavarsha and Other Essays*, express a far stronger consciousness of diversity and difference than of unity or commonality. Further, even if some Sanskrit texts reflect an awareness of cultural commonality among a section of the Brahmanic or Shramanic elite across the subcontinent, that awareness was not shared by the broader population. This elite may have noted recognizable cultural patterns across this land and noted its geographical edges—just as some foreign travellers described the subcontinent as culturally distinct from other lands—but that alone need not translate into a common identity felt by a multitude of its people.

I mean, what we often forgot is that even widely shared cultural practices—such as doing pujas, fasting or going on pilgrimages—need not, by themselves, generate a collective identity or a sense of community. Today, millions of Indians cook curries, play cricket, or wear kurtas—but do any of these activities create a unifying identity or a shared national consciousness? Likewise, a shared set of stories does not ensure a shared identity. Take the case of Biblical lore. Did it manage to produce a significant common identity between the converted Quechua people of Peru and the Spaniards of Valencia? Far from it, because other, larger cultural and structural impediments came in the way.

Such impediments existed all along in the subcontinent. In fact, certain shared cultural practices—such as following the system of varna and jati—actively undermined any potential for a broad-based, inclusive cultural identity. The notion that our ancient ancestors felt a sense of 'unity in diversity' strikes me as a projection of modern Indian nationalism, forged by early twentieth-century Hindu revivalists such as Radha Kumud Mookerji. Claiming ancient roots for this idea essentially served to legitimize their vision of the nation. I wonder why it's almost always Brahmin scholars who see such a unifying 'civilizational identity' (laughs)!

A more cohesive identity sometimes arises in opposition to a well-defined 'Other', but prior to the anti-colonial movement, there was no widely held or stable conception of 'the Other' aligned with subcontinental boundaries. So in pre-modern India, then, we seem to have had multiple, overlapping and shifting local identities, but no sense or basis of a widespread identity or unity, as in 'we are all Indians / one people in this land'.

ROMILA: I haven't come across a clear definition of the entire population, from the lowest to the highest, as Indians in Sanskrit sources.

A wall painting of the Warli adivasis of Maharashtra, depicting dance, music, smoking, campfires, sleeping and various animals in the mix. Photo: Dr Raju Kasambe, CC BY-SA 4.0.

18

Why Didn't Indians Write Travelogues?

NAMIT: Speaking of foreign travellers, I've often wondered why the reverse didn't happen, as in early Indians travelling abroad and writing about other lands, other peoples.

ROMILA: Yes, that's one of the things that bothers me, and I've never understood it. Indians went all over the world in early times, especially as traders. I mean absolutely everywhere: Baku, Moscow, Ethiopia, Yemen, Cambodia, Sumatra, you name it. They had trading settlements all over: some small, some large. You'd think that at least one of them would write a few pages on where he was, what he was doing, whom he met or what the locals were like.

The other thing that bothers me is that Indians don't even write about the various people in different capacities who came to India and wrote about it in any detail. Take the culture of Gandhara in north-western India, which spreads across the Indus into the Punjab. Greek objects of the post-Alexander era have been found, so obviously many more Greeks were settled in these towns than we are even aware of from textual sources. Is there any Indian text that talks about who are these Yavanas (Greeks), what are their practices, what's peculiar about them, you know, the equivalent of Megasthenes? There is no Indian who describes those that come from outside and settle in India. Sanskrit and Greek are close as languages, but no Indian or Greek scholar living in Gandhara recognizes the closeness. There is a brief mention of some non-Indian communities, but it reveals little about who they were as a people and what was their culture.

I can't really explain it. Is it a lack of interest in the other's world, or is it a sense of 'it doesn't matter, they don't matter'? I just find it very odd because normal human curiosity is to say, well, this is what I saw! They don't do it like we do, or they also do it like us, and so on.

NAMIT: Right. Even the Chinese monks, led by their religious quests, still recorded ample social details about Indians—out of sheer curiosity. We seem to have no such Indians. Not only in terms of travelling to foreign lands but also in terms of travelling within the subcontinent and recording different cultures and customs. That's largely missing.

ROMILA: Yes, the villagers must have had some relationship with the adivasis. Mauryan sources and the *Arthashastra* mention the forest dwellers, adivasis bringing forest produce as gifts to the Mauryan administration. Ashoka mentions them in one of his edicts and suggests that they should do what is required of them, else there might be trouble. So there is contact. Why doesn't one of the Mauryan administrators write about the adivasis? Is it just contempt for people not like us? Almost a millennium later, we get an impressionistic account of forest dwellers in *Harshacharita* but no vivid details.

NAMIT: Maybe they saw them as uncivilized beings, or as *rakshasa*s (laughs).

ROMILA: They are all mleccha, so you dismiss them or do little more than mention them. But, you know, is there no intellectual curiosity about why they are living like that, or even thinking differently?

NAMIT: That is a real puzzle. Regular contact with the adivasis has also been indicated by genetic science, which shows small but varying levels of R1a1, or the so-called 'Aryan gene', in the DNA of adivasi groups. These tribal groups lacked caste consciousness, their gods and cosmologies and lifestyles were also very different, yet none of the literate folks seems to have recorded their differences or peculiarities. This despite the trade and the ongoing incorporation of adivasis into the dominant tradition, which would have created proximities conducive to discovery and documentation.

I wonder if one reason might be that writing was very restricted—as in deliberately confined to a small group. Many of them didn't travel overseas for fear of losing caste. Perhaps the culture of this group did not encourage that style of curiosity?

ROMILA: Yes, but then take the Buddhists. They are not really restricted. Yet, there is little description of the society of this Other.

NAMIT: True, and Buddhist traders and monks did go out in fair numbers.

ROMILA: And there is just a little more in their texts about where they are, and what local practices are and so on, but you would think that traders for example, in traders' families, somebody would write a more detailed account.

NAMIT: Could it be that such records were written but were simply lost or destroyed as Buddhism vanished from India?

ROMILA: But then we would have other records referring to them.

a vacuum. There were by now multiple commentaries on the major texts which reflected original thinking, and which continued through the centuries. Perhaps because this was commentarial literature, it tended not to be taken as seriously as the original texts. The second half of the first millennium CE was a high point in philosophical discussion, especially in Buddhist circles. This was curious because it coincided with the edging out otherwise of Buddhism in northern India. It might suggest that patronage for Buddhism declined, or became confined to particular areas, but the intellectual life of Buddhist monasteries did not die. Subsequent to a heightened intellectual challenge of Buddhist philosophers, there was a surfacing of Brahmanical philosophers who questioned the Shramana schools. Was the contention between them becoming more common? A deep comparative study of Brahmanical and Buddhist thought of this period, from a historical perspective, needs to be made. For example, some of his contemporaries and others since then, have suggested elements of Buddhism in the teaching of Shankaracharya, and some commentators on his work have described him as a crypto-Buddhist, which is not treated as an altogether surprising description although it has been debated.

We should also keep in mind that dissenting ideas are necessary to debate and discussion. Where dissent is silenced or quietened down, there will automatically be less advances in knowledge or else the debate will shift to other groups of people. If Buddhism is quietened down in India, the dissent it represents will find an outlet in neighbouring areas or among other sects, as it did historically quit India and move into almost the rest of Asia in the late first millennium CE. But dissent was expressed by others.

The routes opened up by traders were now witnessing the travel of others, some of whom were scholars just visiting India for long or short periods. Indian intellectual centres were in touch with centres such as Baghdad in West Asia and other places in Central Asia. The zero, invented in India, was in circulation and geometry and algebra were initially also attributed to Indian activity. These were being introduced to scholars in West Asia at around the end of the first millennium CE. I had an interesting conversation with George Joseph, who taught history of mathematics in Manchester, and his thesis was that calculus had been discovered by the Sanskrit mathematicians, but some centuries later than the period we are discussing. He maintained that the Jesuits were picking up what they could, and taking it back to Europe, and that was one reason why a century after the discussion of calculus by Sanskrit scholars, the Europeans were familiar with it.

This thesis has not been accepted. But it does raise interesting questions that are worth pursuing. It suggests a churning of knowledge and the emergence of new ideas. Religious missionaries, whether Christian or Buddhist, were perhaps less limited to making religious converts in large numbers because they seem to have been more interested in the intellectual life of those they came across. Chinese and Tibetan Buddhist monks began visiting Buddhist monasteries in India in the later first millennium CE. Their interest lay in learning more about Buddhism and Buddhist thinking on various issues. This is just a small example of what went on over many centuries between groups of people, living possibly in distant places but nevertheless in contact with each other.

We must remember that cultures do not get shaped in isolation. Every culture is partially shaped by the other cultures it encounters and what it imbibes from them, and how it responds to the initially unfamiliar. We in our histories have tended to focus on just one identity, but in effect we have to look at migrations, contacts, interactions—both complementary and hostile. We have to be ready to concede where another may have helped shape us, even if we wish that this did not happen. We have to be willing to grant that there was often a mutually beneficial exchange of ideas.

One of the problems in understanding the history, and more specifically the history of ideas of the late first and early second millennia CE, is that it was the period when the Turks from Central Asia—'Turushkas' in Sanskrit texts—arrived on the scene and, as rulers, kept written records. Modern scholars tend to give more attention to these texts, which, in turn, was influenced by the colonial periodization which argued that with the arrival of 'the Muslims', their texts as the voice of the rulers, adequately described the history of the time. Sanskrit sources, although plentiful, were given less attention and Turkish and Persian texts became the prime sources. The sources were kept segregated although it would have made greater historical sense to have seen whether there was an interaction between them. The Sanskrit and Indian language sources were also reflecting what was going on at other levels of society and, to that extent, their view of social activities is important, especially when comparing it with what is said in Persian and Turkish sources.

We also have to recognize that people from elsewhere were interested in the intellectual activities of Indians. Alberuni (973–1048) was the most outstanding among these. One wishes that Indian scholars had commented on what he had written. We need to analyse more closely what he was viewing and projecting as Indian ideas and activities, and we should compare what he says with what is being written in the Sanskrit sources. For example, Kalhana's *Rajatarangini,* the twelfth-century history of Kashmir in Sanskrit, and Alberuni's India were about a century apart. We could ask whether there are discussions of common factors or diversities in the two books.

One also has to examine the texts of this period not simply from the perspective of the religion of the author but also from the perspective of what they were exploring and writing about. For example, the work of Roberto de Nobili (1577–1656), the Jesuit, was not limited just to making converts to Roman Catholicism. He was in many ways more interested in the thinking of the people he met and the ideas they were propagating. He was not counting the number of converts he made. He was trying to get under the skin, as it were, of those among whom he was living.

I wouldn't call it a decline. It does usher in a change of thought and activity and this needs to be recognized in the context of the historical change in the subcontinent during that period. Every area registers some change. Historiography, for example, begins to be reflected in what was written, such as the royal biographies in Sanskrit and the genealogies that evolved later into the *vamshavalis* (chronicles), in the second millennium CE. We gave this activity low priority because of the arrival and settling in of the Persian and Turkish-speaking rulers. A few continued with their language but many spoke the local Indian language. Akbar and Jahangir were writing poetry in Hindi. There is respect for local learning, and changes in the languages of learning and usage at this time need to be written about. The impact of the coming of Turko-Persian speaking peoples resulted in something new in the Indian royal courts. Did it lead to a decline or just a change?

NAMIT: I think your interpretation on this topic differs from the one I've found more persuasive, so I'd like to understand it better. Many exemplars of learning and innovation you cite, like Dignaga, are however from the mid-first millennium and/or mostly Buddhists, where significant advances indeed took place. And then you cite others from the mid-second millennium, like the mathematicians of the Kerala school from the fourteenth to sixteenth centuries. Whereas I'm referring to a decline in rational-liberal culture and the pursuit of secular knowledge in the Sanskritic strata from the late first millennium. I mean, some biographies and Puranic genealogies written at this time can certainly coexist with a decline in the liberal-egalitarian cultural sphere, right? For example, as Brahmanical orthodoxy surges, the caste system starts becoming more rigid and pervasive . . .

ROMILA: My apologies if I caused confusion. My observations are still based on the late first millennium CE. The mention of the Kerala mathematicians was simply an example of a way of making a comparative point. Buddhism was gradually being edged out in the late first millennium CE and this did have consequences. These, however, resulted in changes in thought and action rather than a decline. Caste, and particularly the upper castes, had worked out rules for the functioning of society. This helped to make the system more rigid—a tendency it was beginning to assert a little earlier too. Where there are rules, these have to be observed. The *Dharmashastras* were putting down the rules and insisting on their being observed. But as with all rules, some were surreptitiously broken. However, they were not broken to a sufficient degree that necessitated changing them.

NAMIT: And as Buddhism, along with its more socially egalitarian ideas, disappears from society by the end of the first millennium in large parts of the subcontinent, a whole way of thinking and being disappears with the demise of Buddhism...

ROMILA: Buddhism disappeared in parts of the subcontinent, but it thrived elsewhere: in Central Asia, China, Japan, Vietnam, Cambodia, Laos, Thailand, parts of Indonesia, Sri Lanka and beyond. In contrast, Hinduism/Brahmanism steadily declined in these areas, mostly surviving in the form of rituals performed by royal courts. Earlier the Shramanic religions had been the agents of dissenting ideas. If Shankara can be called a crypto-Buddhist, then what this suggests is that some Buddhist thought and belief could well have survived in the routine belief and rituals of some important Hindu sects. This needs investigation. There is also the unanswered question that some have asked, namely, what of Buddhism was appropriated by others. Some may cite making the Buddha the ninth avatar of Vishnu, although hardly effectively. We forget that religions did not live behind impermeable walls; they overlapped in segments, borrowed and lent, and there was mixing at many levels, not en masse as a unit.

The decreasing influence of Buddhism in India did not, however, create a void. It was gradually replaced by the rise of a variety of Bhakti sects which did not conform entirely to either Vedic religion or Puranic Hinduism. A bhakta could choose his own deity, form and language of worship, could compose his own prayers, hymns and mythology, and provide his own explanation for why the worship of a particular deity in a particular form was preferred. This was what quite a few did, and it resulted in a vast treasury of texts and poems in the various regional languages of India.

Your suggestion of a decline of the secular and the rational in the late first millennium again raises some complicated issues. Among the philosophical debates of this period are those that examine questions of dissenting from the Brahmanical tradition of thinking. But at the same time, Brahmin authors put together anthologies in support of Brahmanism. One of the more influential of these that refers to the various philosophical schools current at the time, starts with the Charvaka and includes the Buddhists and Jains, so the dissenting groups that supported rational explanations and their ideas, have not been excluded. These are comments on the complicated philosophical views of those times.

It is also possible that we tend to look at the past only in terms of the thought and activities of the elite, whereas what may have stirred people, in the second millennium CE, were the Bhakti saints, and they were not Brahmins for the most part, and were not focusing on Brahmanical concerns. It is often spoken of as one movement—*the* Bhakti Movement—but the regional differences within it are quite substantial.

NAMIT: I agree with that, but I feel like we are describing different aspects of what's happening. So let me restate my position more clearly with fresh details and arguments.

What I'm pointing to is a conservative turn starting in the late first millennium, heralding a decline in the relatively rational, egalitarian and liberal strains of Indian social life, which we more often associate with Buddhism and the Tantric tradition. Such as their anti-caste attitudes and the latter's more strongly anti-patriarchal and sex-positive ethos (a perspective that affirms sexuality as an inherent and wholesome aspect of human life). The Tantric tradition, which had non-Indo-Aryan roots, criticized caste and sati, as in texts like the *Mahanirvana Tantra*. Sure, it was a religion, so it had its share of magical beliefs, but it had a distinct social world view: It was open to all people and actively disregarded notions of ritual purity and pollution. It often venerated fierce goddesses that were independent of male gods, and it had women priests. Rising from the grassroots, it had infused all major Puranic sects during the first millennium, bubbled up notable sites such as Khajuraho and Konark, and also surfaced the elite culture depicted in the *Kama Sutra*. Much of this relatively liberal tradition starts to decline in social life from the late first millennium. Historian Devangana Desai has written insightfully on all of this.

A key figure in these times was Adi Shankara. Certain Brahmin rivals of his day, for their own reasons, called him a 'crypto-Buddhist', but this makes little sense to me. I mean, I'm no expert on Shankara, but what place do things like suffering and compassion and 'no-self' have in his world view? He defended the authority of the Vedas, implicitly endorsing the hierarchical social order based on varna. I see him as a great political rival of Buddhism who shrewdly forged parallel monastic institutions like *mathas*, brought Puranic sects and deities under the theological tent of Advaita Brahmanism, and made this new Brahmanical package more appealing. I think not many historians recognize that the 'triumph' and resurgence of his Advaita world view over Buddhist Madhyamaka (whose chief exponent was the great philosopher Nagarjuna) was *a major regression* in philosophical sophistication. It seems to me analogous to sliding back from Wittgenstein to Kant.

In the late first millennium, we see a feudalism with Indian characteristics, which arguably lowers social mobility as it grows. The number of jatis increase significantly from this time, as more tribes enter the orbit of Brahmanism, bolstering the latter's cultural hegemony. An ever-larger population, including tribal groups who had no experience of caste hierarchy, becomes caste-bound—a long-term setback for egalitarian culture. The practice of untouchability and segregated living rises relative to earlier times, often led by wealthy land-owning temples as the new fulcrum of socio-economic life, including in south India. The once-brilliant tradition of atheistic materialism, of the Charvakas, sadly enters its terminal decline, which is partly why few of their original texts have survived, though sporadic mention of it by theologians continues here and there, as with Madhavacharya.

As the dynasties of the day—Pratiharas, Chalukyas, Rashtrakutas, Chahamanas, Paramaras, Cholas, Pandyas, etc.—turn more Brahmanical, they pull away from Buddhism, and a bit later from Tantra. Warfare between regional kingdoms appears to rise after the Gupta Empire. Most of them also embrace stronger caste positions and observances. For instance, the Brahmanical Sena dynasty in Bengal reintroduced Kulinism in the 1160s—a regressive system of caste and marriage rules—and persecuted Buddhist monks at Nalanda and other monasteries until a lot of them fled south. Royal and aristocratic patronage began shifting from Buddhism and Tantrism to orthodox Hinduism and Bhakti, the two surging games in town, as for example in Vijayanagar. Even in the critiques of caste by certain Bhakti thinkers, such as Basavanna (1131–67), we can see the pervasiveness of caste by the early second millennium—which, I might note, is often also cited as one of many reasons for Islam's appeal to Hindus placed lower down on the caste ladder.

As Buddhism fades and Brahmanical orthodoxy finds greater favour among the elites, caste patriarchy rises too. The plight of women starts worsening, initially more for upper-caste, upper-class women and then trickles down, as elite norms often do. As tribal and Tantric cults get inducted into the Brahmanical pantheon, their female gods keep losing power to male gods. It's notable that nearly all of the gods of the popular *saguna* Bhakti movement are male—forms of Vishnu and Shiva.

The Tantric substrate within Puranic religiosity wanes while Bhakti expressions grow. Erotic temple art, and even the more widespread evocative sculptures of amorous couples on religious sites, decline from the early second millennium in most parts of India. That's a clear trend and what a loss it is! From here on, fewer elites value the *Kama Sutra*, becoming incrementally puritanical. Perhaps not unrelated is that the incidence of sati rises notably in the second millennium among the warrior elites, *especially* in Hindu-ruled kingdoms like that of the Rajputs in the north and Vijayanagar in the south (how many people know that sati was actively discouraged by state authorities in the Mughal realm?). Caste anxieties boost the practice of child marriage for girls, and widow remarriage is increasingly discouraged among the elites. Astrology, witchcraft and divination register notable advances.

In Hindu polities, a perpetrator's caste seemingly shapes what punishment is meted out to him for murder or other crimes. Caste orthodoxy also revives the *kala paani* taboo in many regions—about Hindus losing caste from sea travel—described later by Marco Polo (1292). By then, Arab, Chinese and Indian Muslim sailors have come to dominate the sea trading routes in their dhows and junks. A century later, the Chinese traveller Ma Huan thinks the entire seafaring population of Calicut was either Arab or Mappila Muslim.

Ayurvedic science too has long stagnated, due in part to the reluctance of upper-caste healers, or *vaidya*s—who monopolize formal medical education—to engage with the 'polluting' body and its fluids. The Manu-smriti had demoted the ritual status of physicians who came in contact with sick bodies, a view that apparently revives as Brahmanism grows. Without hands-on experiments, unscientific ideas and practices—based on bodily humours, or *dosha*s—continue ruling Ayurveda, where they stubbornly remain to this day. Instead of cutting their losses, many Indians are today doubling down with AYUSH!

Even the early Bhakti movement—often celebrated for its caste egalitarianism and its non-Brahmanical, even anti-Brahmanical, stance in the poetry of some of its thinkers—is, at its core, a mystical religious movement. It neither elevates empirical understanding, nor is it sex-positive. And its growing popularity draws in Brahmins too, who start appropriating its ideas and forms by embedding them within their own theological framework. A key example is the *Bhagavata Purana*, a tenth-century Sanskrit text that synthesizes Bhakti devotionalism with Vedantic ideas of nondualism, dualism, Brahman and Atman. Later Bhakti saints exhibit a range of attitudes towards the Brahmanical social order. Some, such as Ramanuja, Vallabhacharya, Surdas and Tulsidas, mostly make peace with it. Some scholars hold that despite its diverse regional forms, the Bhakti movement tended to revere the Brahmanical notions of kingship and the divine right of rulers—partly why it attracted royal patronage. So it can be argued that the movement contributed to a more conservative and otherworldly turn within Hinduism.

So these are the sorts of societal changes I'm thinking of in making the case for a conservative turn, which I see marked by a decline in India's liberal, rational, secular and egalitarian cultural spaces—starting centuries before Indo-Muslim rule. By the end of the first millennium, Hindu elites are embracing stronger caste rules, more patriarchy and more puritanical ideas about sex. These social changes begin with them and then trickle down to others in the second millennium.

I know that my condensed overview involves simplifications of the kind that often accompany broad-brush attempts to present a big picture. That said, the conservative turn in sociocultural values that I see unfolding—if at a different pace in different regions—could easily coexist with the rise of new regional states, wealthy elites, royal military exploits or forms of creativity in the orthodox religious sphere that you note: new *Dharmashastras*, commentaries, genealogies, etc. It could also coexist with the dissenting voices of some Bhakti poets, and with pockets of secular creativity, as in prosody and poetics, or in the work of thinkers like Abhinavagupta and Kalhana in Kashmir, and later in mathematics in Kerala—and scattered other examples in what was after all a large territory that, thanks to the land's fertility, hosted around a quarter of the world's population. So my point is: Doesn't all this still describe a decline of sorts whose epicentre is among the Brahmanical elites in the final centuries of the first millennium, and which then spreads more widely?

ROMILA: You are aware of the substantial differences between the society/societies of those times and our own that we are obviously more familiar with. The use of the term 'decline' has many facets as also its opposite, namely, 'advance'. It is perhaps a little difficult to judge an entire subcontinental society as having advanced or having declined. One must examine which facets advanced and which declined, in the many societies that together made up the whole. In the same way, as it is difficult to envisage an entire society having uniformly advanced, it is equally difficult to envisage an entire society having uniformly declined, unless there are specific facets of evidence across a large range of social activities supporting one kind of society from what was there before. If we highlight specific facets—whether philosophical dissent or erotic sculpture—our generalizations should also be correspondingly specific. Advances and declines, after all, are facets of a society that shape its functioning in specific ways, though not always uniformly or across the whole of society. I am a little hesitant to think in terms of such changes coming to entire societies. To me, such changes are more sectional than subcontinental in scope. I would also hesitate to use the term 'decline' to apply to what I perceive as a change—it may be for the better or for the worse—but that has to be judged.

One must also keep in mind regional differences. What you describe is certainly true of a certain part of northern India. Khajuraho, in the middle of Madhya Pradesh, is one example where, in the post-Khajuraho period, the ruling dynasty declined; but in other scattered areas, the decline was more limited or took different forms. Some temples feature distinctive sculptural themes—but how widespread was this? Did they reflect the views of the entire society or only certain segments? Who were the patrons and were these temples accessible to all? A proper assessment must consider how many such temples existed, which sections of society they served, and what demands they were intended to meet. It's not as if the whole subcontinent had a great glory of Tantric sculpture which at a certain moment faded out.

The history of caste and changing caste requires a careful investigation relating it to specific regions, dynasties and other sections of society for which there is evidence. This has not been done by asking the right questions. Small regionalized or localized studies of caste societies in various parts of the subcontinent need to be slotted into an attempt to see the bigger picture. If caste rules could be ignored to accommodate a problematic situation, was this a case of decline or of change, especially if a lower-caste person was being imbued with a higher status? Some might even argue that such examples of upward social mobility were signs of a more advanced society.

Marriages were made between the Turko-Persian nobility ruling the kingdoms of the time, who nevertheless were referred to as mleccha—not having a varna identity—and the local Rajput and other Hindu aristocracy who claimed to be of Kshatriya status. These marriages questioned the rules of exogamy or endogamy that were crucial to caste society, yet they were accepted, based as they were on political power and social status.

Economic development in the second millennium CE has also been discussed. The question of feudalism was tied into the definition given to the post-Gupta grants of land. They gradually increased in number and included both cultivated land and the clearing of waste land. The emergence of large numbers of small kingdoms was not accidental but was tied to these changes. Some dynastic genealogies have been associated with initial grants of land. The economy referred to agriculture and trade, which developed variously. When professional historians even research the nature of society and economy of these times and consider whether or not it can be called a feudal society, they are dismissed as Marxists, although the Marxist definition of feudalism differs! What are we to do?

NAMIT: In speaking of 'decline', I'm mainly referring to the Hindu elites of India—i.e., the Brahmanical strata associated with the dominant ideology of *varnashrama dharma* and its beliefs, values and norms—and what happens to its cultural and intellectual life, and its effects on the rest of society. Scholars speak of declines among other cultural elites, as in the post-Roman centuries of Europe in the second half of the first millennium—what some call 'the Dark Ages', though most scholars now avoid this term. Even there, one can ably argue that not every social and cultural aspect, across every stratum or region, was in decline. The church grew more powerful, its theologians wrote complex exegesis; monarchs boasted military exploits, commissioned grand cathedrals and castles, lived lavishly, etc. And yet, all of this can be said without having to give up the larger point about a decline in the intellectual/liberal/rational streams of elite culture across much of Europe for centuries. I see the situation among Hindu elites in loosely parallel ways, though lasting much longer.

As for Tantric sculptures, they existed all across India, didn't they? These art forms spring from a whole other way of life and thought. We find them in temples in Mathura, Gujarat, Mysore, Badami, Aihole, Pattadakal, Bhubaneswar, Madurai, Konark, Assam, Kashmir and more, although Khajuraho exceeds them all in the density, quality and vividness of the sculptures. Erotic temple art—from playfully amorous Mithuna couples to Maithuna depictions—appears at these and many other places across India for centuries, which starts going out everywhere, especially on temples sponsored by the state and its upper-caste aristocracy and wealthy merchants. That's a significant change.

ROMILA: Yes, there was a sizeable amount of erotic art manifested in temples across much of the subcontinent. But do we understand why this is so? Do we know why there was such an outburst of erotic art after a certain period? It came into prominence in the first millennium CE, so what was the reason? It was not just a fashion since those who donated to and patronized these temples must have asked for it. Were there religious differences as to which deities were associated more frequently with the erotic, were there regional differences, were there differences as to why some sections of society depicted erotic art in particular ways and others in another way or not at all?

It might be useful to plot where various kinds of religious and aesthetic emphases lie. I think a detailed comparative study is called for before we generalize about the subcontinent. In a sense, a kind of erotic symbolism is also evoked in the worship of the Shiva-lingam and that goes back to early times but is not initially identified with the erotic art of the late first millennium CE. What form does it take and what is its purpose and explanation?

Perhaps the question that needs to be asked is whether it was Tantrism in the main that was on the decline. By which I refer to the aesthetics of the temple, its ritual function and the economic resources of the patrons of the temples—the royalty, the aristocracy and wealthy traders. What replaces the earlier theme? Are the donors beginning to put their money elsewhere on other objects and activities? If they're not putting it into Tantric art, are they putting it into other practices? It's not just casteism that's become important. To some extent, yes. The Turks practising another religion and some of them arriving as invaders may have been viewed as a threat to the existing Tantra-infused religion, but at the same time, donations may have been given to other causes.

NAMIT: I'm sorry I'm going on and on about this aspect of cultural change in medieval India, but that's because this question has long obsessed me, and I can't imagine a better person to explore this with. So please bear with me for just a few more minutes.

In trying to understand what elite Hindu society was like around 1000 CE, another great source is *Alberuni's India*. Brilliant testimony, my favourite traveller. And from his account too, it seems that relative to earlier eras, Brahmanical society was less well off in liberal or intellectual terms. It was closing in on itself. Brahmin scholars, Alberuni says, think too much of themselves, though he believes 'their ancestors were not as narrow-minded as the present generation is'. They don't travel anywhere to learn from foreigners, he wrote—something we just discussed. Alberuni has a great scientific and scholarly mind, knows his ancient Greeks; he's a product of a period of scientific, economic and cultural advancement that began under the Abbasids of Baghdad, lasting from the eighth to at least the thirteenth century. Is there a counterpart to Alberuni in the India of that time? I can't think of anyone.

After learning Sanskrit and studying the relevant texts, he notes that the scientific theorems of the Hindus are in a state of utter confusion and are mixed up with all kinds of religious dogmas. The Hindus do not 'raise themselves to the methods of a strictly scientific deduction'. They have even regressed on the great Aryabhata's insights of half a millennium earlier and now believe that the earth does not rotate on its axis and is at rest. Alberuni cites the astronomers Varahamihira and Brahmagupta among this lot—assessing their positions correctly, according to modern historians of science.[17] Keen to spread scientific knowledge, Alberuni even translates for them the books of Euclid and Ptolemy's *Almagest* into Sanskrit. When he starts explaining how to make an astrolabe to study the rotation of the earth, they ask which Hindu scientist he has learned this from! They're like frogs in a well, unwilling to concede that people elsewhere in the world know any science.

Alberuni also describes their social practices, as in the Brahmins refusing to sit with an outsider like him because they fear they might be polluted. He finds that most of them memorize and recite Vedic *shloka*s without understanding their meaning. They refuse to share their special knowledge with members of other castes. Alberuni is a decent man, and he is horrified by the caste system for being the absolute antithesis of both meritocracy and egalitarianism. His account indicates that caste rules by this time were very prominent. He notes that the penalties for a Brahmin eating at a Shudra's home are much greater than the penalties for a Brahmin murdering a Shudra. His account suggests that for Hindu elites, their primary sense of community comes from caste ties. Alberuni's sober documentation of this kind—about actual social practices, law, gender, family, inheritance, etc.—suggests that Brahmanical society has grown insular, insecure, ruled by caste-supremacist ideas. It is turning orthodox. Does this seem like a portrait of intellectual and moral flourishing?

ROMILA: We must keep in mind that Alberuni is writing about a specific segment of Indian society and on specific themes. One can understand Brahmin communities staying close to the *Dharmashastra* rules when speaking to a stranger, but how many other members of Indian society at this time followed the same rules? The number was probably small.

As regards social practice, we also have different stories from other sources. A Sanskrit inscription of the ninth century CE suggests that the rules governing the Brahmins were not always observed by them. The inscription has been read by some as referring to Brahmins being horse traders. The horse trade seems to have involved many Indians of the upper castes. If so, this is an interesting comment on the rules of varna. A Rashtrakuta inscription mentions an Arab who is the governor representing the Rashtrakuta administration in western coastal Gujarat. He bestows a land grant on a Brahmana—surely turning caste a little upside down.

Turning to Alberuni, we have to keep in mind that he confined himself largely to discussion with Brahmins and that too those of a particular region. He did not travel to other parts of India. Had he gone to coastal Gujarat or coastal Kerala, he would have met people who knew and used the astrolabe. His descriptions are therefore a little limited and it is a great shame that he could not spend time in a centre where problems in mathematics and suchlike were being widely debated.

Had Alberuni been based in the Chola kingdom, he would have witnessed other things such as much royal intervention in rituals, manuscripts, travels. He would have been talking about the Chola forces preventing the seas of South-east Asia from becoming a battleground of contesting powers, he would have heard mention of the huge trading guilds such as the Ayyavole 500 and the Nanadesis and the volume of trade. He was not travelling all over India but going to particular places and meeting particular people, and also, he was reflecting the thoughts and actions of only these people. He was not generalizing about non-Brahmin society.

NAMIT: There are certainly instances where the rules of varna were bent by—or on behalf of—Brahmins, particularly when it served their interests, such as in your example involving horse traders. That was an essential aspect of their privilege: custodians of rules often have the power to reinterpret or bend them to their advantage. In your second example, it strikes me that the Arab governor, though a mleccha in varna terms, is in fact reinforcing the caste order by granting land to a Brahmin. Turning caste upside down would have been better achieved with a land grant to an outcaste. So I'm not sure these examples make us doubt the normative hold of caste—or its rising presence—in social life.

Another apparent bending of caste rules you mentioned earlier is Rajput royals marrying their daughters to Mughal princes, who are technically mlechha in varna terms. It seems to me that it took being emperors of India to force this exception in the varna order, when the Mughal imperial family was at the top of the heap. Notably, the reverse did not happen—Mughal daughters marrying Rajput princes—partly because this would have meant 'marrying down', breaking the rules of *pratiloma*, or hypergamy, as Harbans Mukhia has argued.[18] Many Mughal princesses went unmarried not by choice but due to a shortage of mates among their social equals. It's funny how all this works, but I suspect an unsavoury caste logic lurks here too—not surprising among the later, well-assimilated Mughals.

There are other examples of caste rules being 'broken' in which Shudra individuals raised their varna status, usually to Kshatriya, after gaining feudal titles and landed wealth through administrative or military service. Shivaji is often cited as an example of this. The Chandela dynasty, likely of Gond tribal origin, also raised itself to become Chandravanshi Rajputs—aided by Brahmins all too happy to bend the rules for personal gain. Such examples may suggest a flexibility of caste rules, but I wonder if it is best seen as such, or even as a positive feature. Because even here, such 'Sanskritization' of individual families—or of groups who changed their way of life—not only failed to challenge the caste order, but it also strengthened and legitimized it by sanctifying the pursuit of what Ambedkar has called its 'ascending scale of reverence and a descending scale of contempt'.

Does this 'flexibility' suggest a more advanced society? I mean, flexibility in varna rules *could* be seen as a positive feature, but for that, it would help to also cite flexibility the other way, as in Brahmins or Kshatriyas transitioning into Shudras—i.e., true social mobility. A fallen Brahmin might face social ostracism or other penalties from his community, but are there recurring historical examples of his status being downgraded to Shudra? If not—and if only upward mobility was occasionally granted to powerful Shudras—it suggests that the rules and hierarchy of caste were firmly in place, continually reinforced even through exceptions. Some feminists say the same thing about patriarchy and the exceptions it affords a few women (a safety valve?) to better preserve itself.

I'm also thinking of other caste rules that became more rigid in medieval times. Recent genetic data tells us that a momentous change happened about seventy generations ago—so from the second half of the first millennium CE, if we take twenty years as a generation. From here on, says genetic science, strict endogamy is the big norm, 'particularly among Indo-European–speaking upper castes' across much of the subcontinent.[19] Geneticist David Reich estimates that from here on, *not even 1 per cent* of upper-caste individuals marry out of their caste in each generation. This is astonishing if we pause to think about it. From the early medieval period, caste-based endogamy keeps trickling down and infecting an ever-larger number of social and tribal groups across India. I can imagine a lot more inter-caste Romeos and Juliets getting crushed by its rules. That's how we get neighbours of different jatis in Indian villages displaying two to three times the genetic differentiation than between northern and southern Europeans! Genetically, says Reich, India has a large number of small populations.

These findings are quite new, and I think historians are yet to fully explore the questions they raise—not only in terms of how these new norms were so strictly maintained in medieval upper-caste society but also in terms of their impact on felt community and social solidarities, on private lives and personal morality, on creativity and innovation. I fear none of it would look good. This expansion of the caste mindset, flowing down from the elite social strata, is central to 'the decline' I speak of.

As for Alberuni's account, yes, it is about north India. He is mostly speaking about Brahmanical society, but that's also what I am speaking about.

ROMILA: And we are generalizing from his account. He is meeting many upper-caste people. Would he have said the same things if he had gone down to the Deccan and to the south? In the Chola kingdom and suchlike, the social dimensions seem to have been a trifle different. So it's rather a regional thing that's . . .

NAMIT: I agree that Alberuni's account doesn't speak about south India, including the Imperial Cholas, who ruled until the thirteenth century. Perhaps they had more going on, I need to learn more. But I just want to add that huge trading guilds or naval exploits don't refute the 'decline' I speak of. I mean, does the wealth of elites, their armed power or giant temple works accompany humanistic qualities in their culture? The two don't necessarily rise together. To see if the Chola and post-Chola southern elites differed significantly from the northern elites, we should assess the trajectory of humanistic qualities in their culture. Were the differences a matter of degree or kind? Did regressive norms of caste, patriarchy and sexuality not expand during and after Chola rule?

Yes, Alberuni was speaking mainly about Brahmanical society in north India, but that's still noteworthy, right? That's a visible and influential demographic, whose culture had, at least since Aryavarta, trickled down the social ladder and spread to other parts of India—and continued doing so after Alberuni. His account shows the quality of social life and intellectual production among northern Hindu elites on the eve of the Turko-Persian arrivals. His account also seems to align with trends reflected in other historical sources.

On the whole, it sounds like you recognize many changes in Indian society from the late first millennium, though you view them as mixed rather than as marking a decline in the secular, liberal, rational or egalitarian modes of life. But I see a decline radiating outward from Hindu elites—despite the exceptions and regional variations of certain times. Perhaps we are simply framing these changes differently. They strike me as a deepening social malaise. At its heart lay the intertwined pathologies of caste hierarchy and caste patriarchy, corroding our most basic humanity and intimate social relations. These forces may not have operated identically everywhere, but didn't they spread during the second millennium, impacting an ever-larger percentage of the population? In many ways, aren't we still trying to emerge from the long shadow of that past?

I know I'm making some judgment calls. But a few other historians I mentioned earlier have also discussed various kinds of decline in this period, though my arguments have some differences. Nevertheless, I realize this is a matter of debate and I'm interested in other insights that might even change my mind. So I'm grateful to have your perspective. I'm now even more inspired to explore this question further!

Let me just add one final thought—on something that has long bothered me. The thing is that when I look at just the Brahmanical class from the late first millennium onward, I struggle to find their contributions to notable secular-rational knowledge or a humanistic outlook. One could find it earlier in several Brahmins like Panini, Kautilya, Vatsyayana, Kalidasa, Aryabhata, Banabhatta and others—and more if we count Brahmins who quit Brahmanism and became Buddhists, such as Nagarjuna, Vasubandhu, Asanga and Dharmakirti, among others. But in medieval India, even the great engineers appear to have been mostly Shudras, who produced architects, builders, stonemasons, bronze sculptors, wood and ivory carvers, goldsmiths and other skilled professionals and material scientists. Part of the 'Vishwakarma community', these artisans and craftsmen worked in hereditary guilds and built all of India's temple towns, cities and fort-palaces.

What I'm effectively asking is this: In the thousand years before the colonial period, barring rare exceptions, do the men of the Brahmanical castes have an impressive record in advancing the physical sciences, technology, biology, medicine, secular philosophy and art, political thought, or humanism? Do Brahmin men, only a minority of whom were priests, have a distinguished legacy on these fronts, despite their near-monopoly over literacy and scholastic learning? Did all of their knowledge, privilege and access to power and resources produce worthy counterparts to thinkers like Galileo, Gutenberg, da Vinci, William Harvey, Erasmus and Voltaire—or even Alberuni, Alhazen, Ibn Sina, Averroes and Ibn Khaldun—anywhere in India? If not, I think it would be an interesting exercise to explore why this is so and what to make of it.

ROMILA: Part of the reason, and only a part of it, can be attributed to the more secular direction of European thought of a later time. These European thinkers were not products of the Vatican, whether or not they agreed with its teachings. I don't think one can expect an essentially religiously defined social category to be secular. The nuances in the concept of the secular have undergone change. Secularism in earlier times was not contrasted in terms of the material as against the spiritual. Nor was it characterized by the absence of a deity. What it sometimes did refer to, as it does today, is that religion should not control the agencies of governance. This idea that religion and associated beliefs about the supernatural should be a personal matter concerning the individual has become central to society in modern times. It now assumes equality of all members of society and is therefore a substantial support for democracy. Secularism has to be judged by other sections of society and by the general social attitudes prevailing.

Indian society in early times was not secular as the notion of secularity was not a familiar one. Even the Buddhists perhaps were not strictly speaking secular. In later times there was a change. Early Buddhists had not posited the existence of any deity, but deities entered their world later. None of the religions prevalent in India at that time held that religion could not intervene in the creation of social institutions. The Brahmins who produced secular knowledge were not the same as those who performed royal rituals and presided over worship in the temples. I think we have to segregate the scholarly Brahmins from the priests. The latter were obviously not the upholders of secularism.

Humanism is an older idea, but the way we understand it today—as something that permeates society—is a modern concern. The preconditions it requires were weak in early societies.

So looking for the expression of a strong humanism in those days is perhaps a little ahistorical. Still, it is a theme worth exploring.

I also think your insistence on a cultural decline among the Brahmanical classes cannot be used to declare a general cultural decline. The imprint of Brahmanism was also being overshadowed or edged out by other imprints which we need to identify and assess.

NAMIT: Indian society and its institutions, I agree, were not secular in ancient or medieval times. They were religious, but a religious social order can still have qualities and spaces that are relatively more egalitarian, liberal, sex-positive, humanistic and make more room for rational-secular inquiries and creativity, *or* it can be a lot more conservative, patriarchal, puritanical, hierarchical and make less room for rational-secular inquiries and creativity. That a notable shift from the former to the latter—'the decline'—began in the late first millennium CE among Hindu–Brahmanical elites has been my basic argument.

I do take your points about regional differences, insufficient knowledge and the risk of over-generalization. I also see a weakness in my own argument. I mean, in speaking of a 'conservative turn', I sometimes gave the impression of a broad cultural decline. But I don't mean to include the lower-status caste groups or tribes, where the social substrate during this period, it seems to me, often remained more humane, diverse and creative—even as certain problematic trends kept trickling down from the Brahmanical elites.

I also recognize that a society whose elites turn conservative can still be creative in other ways, as you've noted. I may not admire this shift, but others might. For instance, some elites may have viewed the sex-positive traditions of the first millennium CE as degenerate—and welcomed their decline as good riddance. Life surely improved for the votaries of varnashrama dharma as it became the dominant social ideology and drew more groups under its ambit. Men's prospects hardly suffered as caste patriarchy deepened. By other measures—the rise of new states and vocations, expanded trade networks, or innovations in religiosity and architecture—society remained dynamic.

So while I still see a pronounced 'conservative turn', I admit that what I'm calling a decline stems largely from yardsticks that privilege humanistic, secular and liberal values in social life—values I believe to be as old as human societies, if perhaps conceived differently in modern times. But I'll dissociate myself from implying a wider cultural decline, or even stagnation, in other dimensions of social, economic, cultural or religious life. That said, I'm going to think more about this question. I'm so glad we discussed this. Please add any final thoughts, and then shall we proceed to a different topic?

ROMILA: Perhaps I should clarify what I mean by emphasizing the importance of the region. My point is really to draw attention to aspects that historians have often neglected for the period we're talking about—the late first and early second millennium CE, or the Early Medieval period. The political interface continued to be between kingdoms, but there was now also a sharper interface between regions. This arose in part from the much more clearly demarcated identities of the regions. Some languages became the identity of a larger number of people, and so did their literary forms. Regional forms of deities and mythologies appeared in sculpture and painting. Castes were labelled in the vocabulary of varna, but everyday caste practice was often defined more by local jatis, hence the differences in caste observances. Migration from frontier zones into settled areas increased, as did the extension of farming into uncultivated areas through grants of land to individuals and religious institutions.

Regional distinctions were equally evident in religious life, including the diverse forms of Bhakti. Should we see Bhakti as a single, subcontinental movement, or as a multiplicity of religious expressions with recognizable diversities? The Alvars and Nayanars of the Tamil south, for instance, did not have the same identities as Ravidas and Dadu. Jagannath in Orissa, Vitthala in Maharashtra and Krishna in UP had diverse origins. While some concerns were shared, much was also distinct. They may be manifestations of Vishnu yet have different contexts. Some, such as Jagannath and Vitthala, remained regional but Krishna crossed many boundaries. Consent and dissent within Bhakti reflected the specific features of each regional society. This is why I emphasize the regional factor: the Bhakti movements clearly bore regional identities. Their perspectives were not singular or uniform but conformed more closely to the past of each region than to the subcontinent as a whole. Both the regional perspectives and their boundaries can perhaps tell us much about how the localized sense of the past was perceived.

What becomes clear from this intervention is that historical events do not occur in a smooth and level form. History does not move evenly, and the historian has to recognize the changes. I can only repeat what we have said before: that societies are not static, and the changes have not only to be recognized but also explained.

My research on the Somanatha Temple brought home to me the significance of non-Persian sources in constructing the history of the second millennium CE. Because of the Hindu–Muslim–British periodization of Indian history, it was assumed that Sanskrit sources were appropriate for the Hindu period, Persian for the Muslim period and English and European for the British. But in each case, sources in other languages must also be consulted to adequately address the questions that arise from more than a single perspective. In the early medieval period, important texts continued to be written in Sanskrit, as for example those of Abhinavagupta and Kalhana. Such texts must be read not just for isolated nuggets of information but in the wider historical context of the time. Inscriptions are an equally important source, and their significance is increasingly acknowledged. What has received less attention, however, is the integration of such sources into this period's broader history. This may in part be because they are linked not so much to royalty but rather to the elite, both the families of the rich landowners and of the wealthy urban traders and officers of high status.

A Mandana wall painting done by women of the Meena tribe, Rajasthan. Public domain.

20

On Islam's Integration into Indian Society

NAMIT: Another influential narrative in popular history, presented also in James Mill's colonial history of India, goes as follows: Before Muslim invaders arrived from the north-west and established their rule, India was a flourishing and harmonious civilization, a *sone ki chidia* ('golden bird'). Hindu high culture thrived in the arts, sciences, literature, philosophy, etc. The invading Muslims shattered this glorious Hindu civilization, which would otherwise have reached even greater heights.

Mill and other colonial writers, as we've discussed, got much of early Indian history wrong. Contrary to their portrayals—and to later Hindu nationalist fantasies—elite Hindu society in north India, before the arrival of the Turko-Persians, was neither a 'golden age', nor a model of human flourishing. Kingdoms rose and fell amid frequent warfare.

Some Hindus today blame Islam for India's patriarchal norms and sexual prudishness, but that's not historically accurate either. While Islamicate culture had little to commend itself on this front, as in their attitudes to sex, orthodox Muslims and Sufi saints were scarcely different from orthodox Hindus and Bhakti saints. What's clear is that upper-caste Hindus had long cultivated their own patriarchy and sexual puritanism, which, well before Indo-Muslim rule, had been steadily displacing earlier, more sex-positive traditions.

And, as historian Richard Eaton observes in *India in the Persianate Age: 1000–1765*, science in early to mid-second millennium Sanskritic India was 'smugly insular' and 'wilfully ignorant' of developments elsewhere.[20] It was somewhat revitalized through its interactions with the Persianate world, which, some 700–1000 years ago, was in many respects well ahead of both India and Europe. The Mughals catalysed cross-cultural exchanges, translations and extensive record-keeping, which sparked historical thinking, and, according to some scholars, helped induce a nascent, indigenous modernity in some regions—ahead of the more powerful wave of colonial modernity. I think the interactions between the Persianate and Sanskritic worlds were much too complex to be reduced to lazy binaries like 'invader–victim'.

Popular history, however, continues to promote this false idea that Muslim invaders brought down a flourishing Hindu civilization. How do you see the arrival of the Muslims into India and their impact as they slowly become a part of Indian civilization?

ROMILA: To begin with, what do we mean when we talk about 'the Muslims'?

NAMIT: In popular history, Turko-Persians.

ROMILA: Okay, Turko-Persians. Let's first consider the period, from the eighth–ninth centuries to the fourteenth–fifteenth centuries, when western India—especially its coastal region—hosted settlements of Arab sea traders. Indian texts initially refer to them as the Yavanas. As I noted earlier, there's a certain historical continuity in the use of the term. Yavana was originally used for the Greeks. The term 'Yona' was derived from 'Ionia', the back formation being Yavana as used in Sanskrit. So anyone coming from the west was called Yavana. Even Queen Victoria was occasionally referred to as a Yavana Maharani.

The traders that came to India from West Asia, the eastern Mediterranean and East Africa were also called Yavanas since they came from the west, although they were Arabs. This trade dates to the turn of the Christian era prior even to the rise of Islam, from Roman times of about the second century BCE to the early centuries CE. Those living on the southern coast of Arabia and Yemen, extending as far as Egypt, maintained long-standing contacts with the west coast of India. This commerce has been described variously as Indo-Roman trade, Mediterranean trade, or Red Sea trade—overlapping networks that together created a vibrant web of exchanges. These traders had established economic bases in India along the west coast from Gujarat to Kerala, and in some cases extending to Sri Lanka. The Khojas, Bohras, Navayaths and Mappilas are communities that evolved from such early Indo-Arab settlements. The trade continued even after the conversion of the Arabs to Islam. Over time, they developed distinct religious traditions that diverged from standard doctrinal forms. The Khojas and Bohras, for instance, evolved belief systems that cannot be neatly classified as either Islam or Hinduism; rather, they represent hybrid traditions shaped by elements of both. The Muslim Mappilas were expert seafarers and merchants, spoke Malayalam, and some of them practised matriliny. These traders communicated in Arabic, Greek and Prakrit languages. Some among these Yavanas were well settled in western India, such as those that held administrative jobs under the Rashtrakuta rulers.

The other later category of Muslims are the Turushkas, the Turko-Persians of Central Asia who spoke Turkish and Persian. They hovered in the north of India, trading but waiting to invade because clearly the trade was very lucrative and controlling the region where it flourished would bring in greater profits. Not all Turko-Persians were invaders since there were large groups of migrants among them who were pastoralists and some were traders, as also a large number of Sufis of distinctive religious orders who settled in India. So to refer to Muslims as a uniform, all-inclusive category is historically inaccurate because in terms of their culture there are at least two categories of them initially and they grow to more.

NAMIT: You're absolutely right—people often forget about this older category of Muslims in south India that you've just described. In popular history, Muslims are largely equated with Turko-Persians coming from the north-west, and they're seen exclusively as invaders and destroyers. But somehow such monochromatic assessments aren't applied to others *within* the subcontinent. I mean, Ashoka invaded and destroyed Kalinga. The Pallavas overran the Ikshvaku kingdom. Rajendra Chola I led devastating invasions of regions leading up to the Gangetic plains. The Maratha cavalrymen, the Bargis, invaded and pillaged Bengal for a decade. Yet, popular history doesn't brand these figures as 'invaders' and 'destroyers', saving these terms only for the Turko-Persians. Popular history also has little interest in dwelling on how both the guest and host cultures were shaped by a complex dynamic of migration, conflict, mixing, coexistence and cooperation.

ROMILA: Popular history also misses out on the fact that the folks that came from the north-west initially came south as far as the Vindhyas and then paused. Some of them established kingdoms that were technically Islamic because the ruling dynasties were Muslim, but they ruled over large non-Muslim populations. The Muslim in the peninsula was not identical with the Muslim of the north, the Yavanas were not the same as the Turushka. The south, like the north, was strongly Vaishnava and Shaiva at this time. But southern politics had various dimensions absent in northern India. These I have already referred to but let me repeat it for emphasis. The trading groups, with the political concession of the Cholas, were asserting their presence in Southeast Asia and were impressively wealthy. Their economy had to accommodate the growing demands of commerce with powerful guilds like the Ayyavole 500, the Manigramam and the Nanadesi controlling so much of the exchange across the peninsula and overseas. This southern part of the Indian subcontinent had little to do with the Turko-Persians until somewhat later. The familiarity with the Muslims here was more with the Yavanas and later with the Sufis. The Cholas ruled until the thirteenth century followed by the return of the Pandyas, who established their dynasty emerging from the conflicts with the Hoysalas and Eastern Chalukyas. Not that the commercial economy of the north was insignificant. Indian imports of horses from Central Asia, in return for textiles, were substantial. So the functioning of large-scale economic organizations had their counterparts in the various regions of India. They were dominant in some places and less so in others. What deserves closer attention as a cultural and religious idiom is the emergence of distinct regional expressions of Bhakti during a period when political power was shared among both Hindu and non-Hindu rulers.

The incoming Turko-Persians practiced various occupations as is common among migrants. The popular generalization is that 'the Muslims' came only as conquerors, hence the antagonistic relations with the local host society. In reality, migrants from Central Asia, once settled, became part of the social fabric—pastoralists, for instance, virtually merged with the host society—while others, such as craftsmen and traders, asserted themselves in various ways yet still became broadly integrated. The use of common caste names, however occasional they may be, does suggest that some identities were close.

Shepherd communities from Central Asia trickled in. They came from an area where Buddhism was in decline and Islam was beginning to get a foothold. They moved to areas where they set up or joined cultivating communities. Herders were good transporters and were proficient in moving horses to large trade centres. The Turko-Persian-Indian trade, with horses coming into India and textiles going out, was a substantial part of the exchange economy. Smaller items also found their markets. The trade helped north India flourish as indeed the maritime trade of the same period brought wealth to the south. Doubtless, the image of wealth conveyed by these activities attracted the attention of those looking for wealth and it brought in groups willing to acquire it through conquest.

So those seeking kingdoms and alliances gathered a small army together with groups of mercenaries and essentially carried out large-scale raids with an occasional battle. The earlier ones came through Ghazni and Ghor and gradually other routes opened up. Travelling through the Punjab from Delhi to Amritsar, a striking feature to this day is the number of caravanserais and little mosques of this period that dot the landscape, all with early Turko-Persian-Indian features. Some caravanserais are huge and impressive, and one can almost sense the domination of traders, whereas earlier there might have been more royal palaces.

Invasion may have been seen as a way to acquire more territory but probably conditioned by the question of how best to control trade and extract greater wealth from it. The Turko-Persians of Central Asia—'the Muslims' identified in Sanskrit sources as the Turushkas—already dominated the major trade routes and market centres. The label Turushka, much like Yavana, has a layered history: Kalhana's Rajatarangini, an eleventh-century history of Kashmir, even refers to the Central Asian Kushans as Turushkas. Doesn't this reflect a sense of historical continuity of people arriving from particular regions for various reasons to settle in India? Speaking of migrations, it is worth remembering that both pastoralists and traders qualify as migrants when they leave their homelands. Migration and settlement reflected a blend of motives—some seeking new outlets for their economic activity, others attempting to dominate and control those activities through conquest.

NAMIT: You mentioned the Sufis among those who came. I think popular history also fails to recognize how much the Sufis and their message of social equality, brotherly love and social service helped to domesticate Islam in the subcontinent—especially in the Deccan and the Bengal frontier—and to make it attractive to many Hindus of the lower castes. Their attitudes of devotionalism were akin to Bhakti. I find it fascinating that it was the Sufis of the Chishti order who introduced the concept of langar in the subcontinent, i.e., free daily community kitchens, where lay volunteers cooked not just for those of the faith but for anyone and everyone to sit and eat together, regardless of one's caste, class or religious background. This was later institutionalized in Sikhism but—not surprisingly—did not resonate with the Brahmanical ethos, which saw a large proportion of fellow humans as 'polluting' and barred them from even entering its prominent temples, let alone eating in their precincts. The idea of breaking bread with 'untouchables' horrified the Brahmins. This was the case in most big Hindu temples across India until recent times, such as Varanasi's Vishwanath Temple, Puri's Jagannath Temple, Kerala's Sabarimala Temple, Tirupati's Sri Venkateswara Temple and Madurai's Meenakshi Temple.

Then there was another category of people who came: refugees. One such moment arose when Genghis Khan—a follower not of Islam but of Tengrism, a shamanistic religion—ravaged many parts of Central Asia in the early thirteenth century. Many people, like Amir Khusrau's father in Samarkand, fled and sought refuge with the sultan in Delhi (later sultans repelled multiple Mongol incursions into the subcontinent). There was also the category of economic migrants who came looking for opportunities, like today's Indians going to the Middle East or Silicon Valley. Many of them sought work in Indo-Muslim administrations—in Delhi, Agra, the Deccan. Many settled there and were assimilated like previous comers.

One such example is Daneshmand Khan, a nobleman in Aurangzeb's court, who also employed the French physician François Bernier for almost a decade. Khan had come from Persia and worked as the Mughal secretary of state for foreign affairs and grand master of the horse. Bernier warmly called him 'my Agah' (chief, master), 'the most learned man of Asia', 'whose thirst for knowledge is incessant' and who voraciously read works on astronomy, geography, anatomy, the materialist philosophy of Gassendi, Descartes and more. Khan's scientific curiosity led Bernier to cut open living goats and sheep to illustrate to him the principles of the circulation of blood, recently explained by William Harvey. Khan, it seems to me, represented a whole new kind of urbane intellectual in India at that time. So yes, many categories of people came for various reasons.

ROMILA: What I'm trying to highlight as well is that migrants to India often brought, or adopted, many different occupations—not just warfare. To focus only on invaders and conquerors gives us a skewed view of history. Every invasion involved not just warriors but a wide range of people—traders, artisans, stable hands, porters, hakims, cooks and others—many of whom were curious about the perhaps unfamiliar society they had entered. When we picture an invasion, we need to imagine more than just soldiers; we should see an entire mobile community. *The Harshacharita* gives us a glimpse of this, describing Harsha's army as resembling a small township on the move. Warfare itself was organized very differently from our times. It's also important to remember that, even before the Islamic period, the subcontinent had already seen centuries of battles, violence and large-scale slaughter.

NAMIT: Yes, that's always worth keeping in mind. The incoming Indo-Aryans too must have included a variety of types, as did others who subsequently came to settle in India, such as the Austroasiatic peoples (Munda, Khasi), Scythians/Sakas, Kushans, Ahiras, Huns, Tibeto-Burmans (Naga, Bodo-Garo, Meitei, Kuki-Chin, etc.). From the eight and nineth centuries onward, Arabs, East Africans, Turks, Persians, Afghans, Uzbeks, Southeast Asians and others entered India. Their diverse cultures and identities became fertile ground for both conflict and creativity in the subcontinent. Each encounter brought its share of tension and misunderstanding yet also sparked curiosity and mutual fascination. In due course, each group assimilated, becoming as Indian as any other and adding its distinct flavours to the salad bowl of Indian culture.

This process is far from unique to India—it is a global pattern. We are, after all, a migrant species. Take the much smaller land of Britain, for instance. By 1200 CE, it had already absorbed many waves of newcomers: the first hunter-gatherers, neolithic Anatolian farmers (who built Stonehenge), the Bronze Age Bell Beaker people (of Steppe ancestry), Celts, Romans, Angles, Saxons, Jutes, Vikings/Norse and Normans—each causing shifts in language, religion, customs and a range of material technologies. As in India, historical understanding of these migrations has evolved significantly in Britain. Whereas older historiography portrayed the Angles and Saxons as invaders, modern archaeology, linguistics and genetics point instead to a slower, multi-generational migration of both sexes, marked by peaceful settlement, intermarriage, cultural blending and occasional violent conflict. Even the incoming Norse, long caricatured solely as raiders and warriors, are now also recognized as farmers, fishermen, traders, shipbuilders, textile makers and other skilled artisans.

I think it's worth recognizing that even as the Turko-Persians, like other incoming groups, introduced new social stresses and conflicts, they also enriched Indian culture in numerous ways. Who can say what a counterfactual history without them might have looked like—it may well have yielded a less cosmopolitan and more hierarchical culture, no? Yet today's popular history and Bollywood seem unable to see the Turko-Persians as anything other than villainous invaders—turbaned Islamic hordes on horseback, dark beards, greedy kohl-lined eyes, all guns ablaze, so to speak (laughs). I won't bet on that caricature changing anytime soon.

A Pithora painting of the Bhils and Rathvas of MP and Gujarat (Museum of Man, Bhopal). Photo: Namit Arora.

21

What's Pride-Worthy in the Hindu Past?

NAMIT: Let's now shift to a very different topic. In today's world, most people just *luuuuv* to take pride in their cultural past. Personally, I find it hard to take pride in things I did not help create—such as the accident of birth into a particular community or territory. That said, I also recognize that if I were inclined to seek pride in such inheritances, I would find plenty in Indian culture to inspire it.

Yet, too many Hindus today bypass the real and prefer to take pride in fantasies of an imaginary Hindu past. Their desire for cultural pride leads them to accept myth as history or partake in historical distortion. That's unwarranted of course, but it's interesting that some Hindus also feel a sense of unwarranted shame. An anguished woman recently asked me the following question online. How would you have responded to her?

> 'Is there a single thing in the last 3000 years of history that Hindus should be proud of? Or do we just have to be ashamed of everything? Can you please talk about some things that Hindus can be proud of?'

ROMILA: Well, there's much superb Sanskrit literature, and poetry and drama which is not taxing to read. It has also been translated. There is scientific writing, but this may be a little tough to understand and some describe it as protoscience. Most Indians don't take the trouble to familiarize themselves with the real thing, so they get fobbed off with fake statements. So how can they begin to be proud of that? It is said that both algebra and geometry evolved through Indians advancing them. Zero and the decimal number system were used in India around the seventh century CE. These are really important.

NAMIT: You know, zero is especially dear to me. I grew up in Gwalior, which has the earliest-known epigraphic evidence of zero as a part of decimal notation! Or at least the earliest that's on stone, found at a Vishnu temple on a path going up its hill fort. I do take pride in associating myself with zero! (laughs) But yeah, early Indian maths is quite impressive. Can you speak more about things in the cultural realm?

ROMILA: That is the cultural realm for me!

NAMIT: Right, doing science and maths are aspects of human culture too! But you know what I mean.

ROMILA: Alright, in the cultural realm, such as architecture, art, literature and religion. We tend to look at the end product and judge it. We seldom consider the equally important question of who made it. We should recognize the first-rate craftsmen evident from the great stupas and temples of old and from Mughal architecture and regional styles, built by some local craftsmen and some migrants. These were the *shilpins* (artisans), who helped build them and kept them in good repair as their inscriptions inform us. The Turushkas did not bring large numbers of craftsmen because they did not need to. Just a few were sufficient and Indian craftsmen were excellent. It was the same with the court artists, the larger number were local painters and were trained by the elders among the artists.

Let me illustrate this by quoting four or five inscriptions from the Qutb Minar, inside the Minar as you go up. They're inscriptions written in Devanagari, composed in poor Sanskrit, by masons with Hindu names, who were called in the fourteenth century by Feroz Shah Tughlaq to repair the Qutb Minar. It had been struck by lightning. A group of them came and recorded the repairs they carried out as well as their names, adding that they succeeded in doing the work because they had the blessings of Vishvakarma; they write, '*Shri Vishvakarma prasade rachita*' or 'Executed with the grace of Vishvakarma'. This is inside the Qutb Minar.

These craftsmen, trained in another architectural tradition, quickly adapted their techniques—with the help of the god of craftsmen, Vishvakarma! It shows that they were really accomplished, adapting to the new style but also retaining something of the old. The quality of their work is what we should be proud of, as also the aesthetics of the art and the architectural style. We should also recognize that a building may be named after a patron who provided the wherewithal, but the actual workmanship came from the craftsmen. Are the authors of the cultural objects the patrons or those who actually made them?

We have become used to describing civilization as a unique expression of the elite of a particular society and our understanding of what goes into its making is often confined to the cultural patterns of the imaginings of the elite. But in viewing it thus, we miss out on two other important aspects. One is that those who actually construct the objects that define a civilization are people we frequently overlook, such as the artisans and craftsmen. There are of course paintings and books that are products of a single person, but other creations may have manifold makers. And second, we take civilization to be a well-protected formulation from the single source of society with which we associate it. But in fact, when we take apart the making of ideas and objects that have been essential to civilization, we find that its form is porous and it integrates other elements from cultures that interact with it.

So when someone asks what we should be proud of in our culture or rather in our varied cultures, it does lead one in many directions.

NAMIT: Yeah, certainly. I don't know this woman, but I suspect her question was implicitly about taking pride in Brahmanical Hinduism, which she seemed to feel defensive about. That is, after all, what most people mean by 'Hinduism'. For me, this elite layer and subset of Hinduism is indeed harder to take pride in, since it has historically been bound up with caste supremacy, patriarchy, the asocial and self-centred ethics of moksha, disdain for manual labour, purity–pollution taboos and colonizing cultural instincts. However, one can still appreciate its theological non-dogmatism, its relative syncretism, and the intellectual achievements of many individuals in it. But this otherwise baneful layer of Hinduism should never be conflated with the whole of Hinduism.

However, if we take all of the groups now included in the constitutional idea of 'Hindus' and consider their ancestors, then we suddenly have a lot more ideas worth taking pride in. We could begin with the Harappans and their amazing urban planning, including indoor toilets and city-wide drainage, and in their being substantially egalitarian and non-warlike. In this, they seem far ahead of the Egyptians and the Mesopotamians. Then there is the great diversity of 'Hindu culture' and its rich storytelling traditions. Adivasi groups, such as Gond, Santhal, Bhil, Baiga, Khasi, Munda, Warli, Naga, Irula and others have a rich repertoire of creation stories, mythic epics, heroic ballads, folk tales and ancestral legends, often preserved through song, dance, music, rock paintings and other visual art. We once had thousands—and still have hundreds—of languages in the subcontinent, each representing a somewhat different way of describing and relating to the world. We also have remarkable traditions of musical ragas, folk music and dance, flute and percussion, complex theatre with ancient roots, and more.

Or consider the ecologically minded knowledge systems of the adivasis, and their ways of conservation and sustainable management of forests, wildlife, soil, water, land and other natural resources. Or the egalitarian and matrilineal customs of folk culture that once gave women more equality. Or take the quality of Shudra artisans, architects, bronze and stone sculptors, who worked in guilds and passed down their sophisticated knowledge of materials, metallurgy and artistic design. These skilled manual labourers from a host of 'Vishvakarma communities' used their bare hands and simple tools to build so many of Hindu India's marvellous temples, forts and cities—as well as Mughal buildings!

Also pride-worthy is the religious pluralism of so many of our Bhakti saints and the reflective spiritual traditions of meditation and renunciation. Or take the sexual liberalism of the grassroots Tantric substrate, out of which arose a substantial sex-positive culture during the first millennium, producing the *Kama Sutra* and all that amazing temple erotica. Those lovey-dovey couples in stone that once adorned so many of our religious buildings are so charming and unique! Really, there's no shortage of wondrous things in Hindu India's past.

ROMILA: Also consider the old miniature paintings by Hindu and Muslim artists, whether working under the Mughals or in the scatter of Rajput kingdoms co-existing with the Mughal empire. And the exquisiteness of that painting tradition is something that more of us should learn to appreciate because it is quite remarkable! Many of the top artists in the Mughal courts were Hindus. And they bring some of the earlier tradition from the Jain manuscripts into the Mughal tradition apart from the Mughal style into the paintings at the lesser courts. So that's something else that we should be proud of . . . if we're looking for elite cultural objects.

And again, this is not something that's usually regarded as high culture, but in my opinion is very much that. Let's consider weaving techniques for which we were held in great esteem by the rest of the world. It's absolutely brilliant what our weavers achieved. We could hold the world to ransom so to speak. The trade that went on with Indian textiles, in every direction, was huge. The economy of India was flourishing partly because it was importing horses that, it was claimed, sweated blood—they were said to have come from Ferghana—and it was exporting large numbers of exquisite textiles, whether of cotton, silk and various mixtures, including chintz, muslin, chanderi and other fabrics.

Another thing we must appreciate is the vibrant culture of dissent that existed in our past. This dissent, expressed through disagreement on various subjects, manifested both as public opinion and in more formal debates. It reflected a certain culture of non-conformity and an acceptance of difference. Dissent was not limited to the *nastika* (or *Shramana*) traditions; it was equally prevalent among the many sects within Hinduism. In fact, dissent often served as the catalyst for the emergence of new sects that offered alternative world views. The subject of dissent—its diverse forms and social impact—deserves far greater attention and deeper analysis from historians today.

NAMIT: Yes, that's a great point. Making fine textiles requires great imagination! Even ancient Kashi was famous for its textiles—as modern Kashi still is, even in our age of automation. So this amazing tradition is quite old.

Alright, I think that's a pretty good list of things from our history that our anxious Hindu woman could consider taking pride in. Of course, if she were instead looking to take pride in being 'Indian', the scope of pride-worthy things would jump notably!

Wall painting drawn if a female priest dies, Saora Tribe. Display at Tribal Museum, Koraput, Odisha.
Photo: Namit Arora.

22

On the Promise and the Perils of Nationalism

NAMIT: Having considered pride in a particular cultural identity, let us now turn to pride in a particular nation—that is, nationalism, which has also become widespread today. Most scholars regard concepts such as the nation, nationalism and the nation-state as relatively recent, rooted in the experience of modernity. They are generally seen as having first taken shape in Europe before spreading to other parts of the world. How do you understand the origins of these powerful ideas of the nation and the nation-state?

ROMILA: In the eighteen–nineteenth centuries, parts of Europe experienced rapid social, economic, technological and cultural change, accompanied by new ideas that we now associate with modernity. People began questioning hereditary kingdoms and authoritarian rule. They thought of alternative social structures and forms of government. There was a growing hunger for popular sovereignty and a new basis for organizing political communities.

This drew many to the new concepts of the nation and nation state, in which many categories of people could draw on a sense of common heritage based on a commonality of languages, customs and religions that had long coexisted. People recognizing such a shared heritage came together to pursue new forms and patterns of life, pre-eminently the belief in the liberation of the individual, democracy as essential to the functioning of a society and secularism ensuring that social control did not lie in the hands of an organized religion.

There were many other concurrent social changes. Agriculture's centrality to the economy was being replaced by industrialization and more intensive commerce. The old aristocracy and feudal hierarchy were being replaced by a new class of individuals with access to money and power associated with it. Growing scientific knowledge and discoveries began creating new ideas of the self, new vocations and lifestyles. The liberation of the individual gave authority to the individual. These new ideas were spread and domesticated through growing literacy, newspapers in circulation and other print media. The difference lay not only in these individual items that changed but in the larger change that introduced the idea of a nation and the bringing together of people in a nation state. In the changed society that results from nationalist thinking, there is also the recognition of a new identity.

NAMIT: That makes sense—those new conditions clearly contributed to the rise of nations and nation states in Europe, driven by regional nationalisms. Political scientist and historian Benedict Anderson has explored this vividly in *Imagined Communities: Reflections on the Origin and Spread of Nationalism* (1983), where he famously described nations as 'imagined communities'. If we define nations as such and see nationalism as something that binds people in a shared identity, then there can be many ways of achieving it—not just the ideal way you've outlined. I mean, while secularism can be central to nationalism, religion can be too. Both can be used to forge a sense of collective belonging, right?

ROMILA: I believe secularism must be central to nationalism in societies with multiple religions, such as India. Nationalism, after all, is meant to unite all members of society—not just those from a single religious community. To be successful in forming an imagined community out of a diverse population, it has to be truly inclusive. The thrust of nationalism has to be broad enough to embrace both the religious and the non-religious alike. Moreover, secularism is not just about ensuring equality among religions; more fundamentally, it demands freedom from religious control and advocates a clear separation between religion, social institutions and the State.

Nationalism, in this sense, must be both democratic and secular—not because these terms have fixed, singular meanings but because nationalism necessarily involves diverse groups coming together to shape a shared national identity. Since nationalism arises at the intersection of many identities and experiences, it cannot—and should not—be based on a narrow idea that excludes many. That is the recipe for a failed nation.

NAMIT: So true. That recipe has produced failed nations in our own neighbourhood, and we seem to be heading on that path too! Earlier in our conversation, you called yourself an 'old-fashioned nationalist'. I see now that behind that term is your vision for the kind of nationalism you've just outlined: secular, democratic, liberatory to the individual.

I sometimes use a different way to reason about this with people. I employ the thought experiment that John Rawls discussed in *A Theory of Justice* (1971). He invited readers to a thought experiment he called the 'veil of ignorance'. He asked them to imagine creating 'a hypothetical social contract in an original position of equality'. Imagine, he says, that 'when we gather to choose the principles [for governing ourselves], we don't know where we will wind up in society. Imagine that we choose behind a "veil of ignorance" that temporarily prevents us from knowing anything about who we are', including our race, caste, gender, class, talents, intelligence, wealth, religion, etc. Imagine that we are a spirit waiting to be born randomly to somebody in the world. What principles would we then choose to order our society? Rawls makes a powerful case that simply out of a desire to minimize our odds of suffering, we will always choose political equality, fair equal opportunity, secular governance and an egalitarian social order. This view has been crucial to the debate on reducing ascriptive social inequalities—of caste, race, gender and more.

Many thinkers, however, see much less promise in the project of nationalism, with the real world often proving their point. They long to transcend nationalism, though it's less clear what might replace it. Their many complaints against nationalism include: (1) it invariably makes up a story of the nation's past that is full of invention, exclusion and exaggeration; (2) its quest to forge a common identity is corrosive to diversity; (3) it fuels xenophobia and competitive rivalries among nations; (4) its strongest supporters tend to be social elites who, according to Eric Hobsbawm, use nationalism and national identity as tools to advance their own class interests, while projecting them as national interests—a clever trick! (5) nationalism serves to prioritize these 'national interests' over basic human needs and solidarities, which raises social strife as well as impedes cooperation on global issues like climate change.

Tagore famously disliked nationalism and saw it as a kind of idolatry and pathology imported from Europe. In his 1917 essay 'Nationalism in India', he wrote, 'Nationalism is a great menace. It is the particular thing which for years has been at the bottom of India's troubles'.

What would you say to such critics of nationalism?

ROMILA: Well, first of all, let me indulge in an oversimplification. I see nationalism as the articulation of a particular kind of historical change. I mean, if one takes the example of India, there were states of various kinds, largely kingdoms, and then there was colonial rule and a colonial state. The hostility to the colonial state was because of its oppressive character. Indians did not want to be a colony of an empire. Many began longing for self-rule, rights and democratic governance.

What is a nation state? It is defined as a territory whose people get together and say, we have much in common, we have the same aspirations, so we should form a nation. And so the movement starts, the colonial power is removed, a nation state is established. There is a given territory, and a variety of people come together. How are they going to be brought together? It cannot be done via claiming the same identity in any one of the following: religion, ethnicity, language or suchlike. It cannot be a singular identity based on any of these as that would eliminate the coming together of the various kinds of people in a given territory. So how do you make it viable?

There are certain givens of a nation state that distinguish it from the kingdom and the colony. The nation has to be a structure that guards the rights of all citizens. Citizenship becomes the pivotal component—a complete change from the lack of it in earlier forms. It is really a major historical departure. And when I say I'm an old-fashioned nationalist, it's because I believe that the future of the world lies in nation states that are governed by citizens who have rights and that the governing has to be essentially democratic and secular. Which is not always the case with nation states today.

I don't regard the modern nation as something that has come to us from the West and has therefore to be discarded. I think it's a part of our historical evolution. And it is linked to the world of today. Colonies, when they cease to be that, move towards becoming nations. When one has been controlled by a highly centralized system and governed very strictly, one longs for the liberation of being a free citizen. This comes by having a nation state that is democratic and secular and gives everyone citizenship rights.

NAMIT: How do you then respond to Tagore's critique that the nation, deep down, is based on a kind of idolatry that's often evident in its symbols, such as the flag, the anthem, monuments, sacred soil and borders, invocations of a glorious past, and so on?

ROMILA: I think there are two phases of nationalism. At one level, getting everybody together. How do you get them together? Flags, slogans and so on. At another level, a nation needs larger ideas to unite people, including a shared vision of the past and of the future. That sometimes gets diverted, as in this country, into majoritarianism, religious nationalism. It can have other downsides that its critics fear, especially if the nation's social elites do not lead in a responsible way. When we start qualifying nationalism and commit ourselves to religious nationalism, linguistic nationalism or ethnic nationalism, then we are done for. Because it then takes the form of the dictatorship of that specific group in the name of majority rule. In such a situation, secularism is excluded and so is democracy. True nationalism has to be something where democracy and secularism are fundamental. Absolutely fundamental. There's no way in which anything should divert us from that. Only then can we have a state in which people are liberated. Then one can make demands on the state, to provide the kind of society we want. I don't know whether that will happen here.

NAMIT: Okay, so the exemplary nation state has citizens organized in a secular democracy. But who gets to try and set up a nation state? You said that it happens when people in a territory get together and say, we have much in common, so let's form a nation state. Now, it's one thing for some people at the top to make that claim, quite another for it to be supported by *actual* commonalities or a broadly shared identity or sense of the past. What attributes of culture and identity do you think we had in common in the 1940s that justified India becoming a nation state?

I mean, what common, unifying ideas were shared by Tamils and Mizos, or Brahmins and outcastes, or urbanites and adivasis, or nawabs and peasants, or maulvis and pandits, or Goans and Kashmiris, or Khasis and Marwaris? We had no common language. What we did have was a tactical and temporary unity for the cause of expelling the British, but this sense of unity was bound to fade afterwards, as it arguably did. Were there any deeper commonalities that justified the idea of a nation state in a territory that had rarely, if ever, been politically unified, nor had a sufficiently unifying cultural identity felt by its people?

ROMILA: The commonalities were not in these individual expressions that you have listed but rather in the more general idea of combating people with altogether different ambitions and whose identity was different. It was the sense of a new experience of coming together to create a nation. Even the definition of a nation was not too clear at that time, and this may explain why people with various ideas were at times coming together and at times breaking away. The main thrust was anti-colonialism and the precise definition, of who and why there was a nation in opposition to colonial control, remained rather vague.

When I take a long historical perspective on the subject, I do tend to see the nation state as an intermediary to some other form—hopefully a completion of the requirements of a functioning nation. What will follow remains unclear. Large territories may break up into smaller ones, smaller ones may battle against each other or a new form of organizing a state may emerge. Nationalism achieved its purpose and established nations. I don't know what form they will take as they evolve.

NAMIT: Benedict Anderson saw nationalism as filling the void left behind by the relative loss of religion in a secularizing age. Nationalism, as he sees it, stepped in to serve similar psychological and social needs as religion. And it did so by cultivating an alternative sense of identity and social order, a new sense of the past, new stories about the 'national community', a new moral framework of duties to the nation with its own ideas of sacrifice, loyalty and service. Nationalism is based on the fiction of 'a national community', an in-group that exists only in our imagination (after all, we don't actually know the vast majority of those said to be part of 'our community'). Nationalism employs an alternative set of rituals and symbols: national holidays, awards, parades, flags, anthems, heroes, martyrs, statues, etc. Both address the human need to belong to something larger than oneself—something meaningful and seemingly enduring. What do you make of the critique that nationalism shares certain features with religion—including its downsides?

ROMILA: The problem is that in some societies, nationalism has been explicitly conceived in religious terms by saying that religion is fundamental to our lives. But it's really what you do to an ideology. I think it's something that will face a crisis when people have to weigh up the priority of religion with that of the citizenship of a nation. It is a choice that has been faced in recent history by the Jews in Nazi Germany and often by minority groups in Asian and African societies in our times. It's a problem many societies are facing today.

One of the challenges with bringing people together is that they have to be convinced that they share a culture. And even more, that they share a history. Even if they are migrants or come from non-elite groups, they have eventually to internalize a shared history. This requires some creativity and integrity from the social elites. Religion has a role in many people's lives, but I would say that the ultimate purpose of nationalism is, or should be, to liberate the individual and to give the individual a chance to live a decent life.

NAMIT: That's also the purpose of classical liberalism, which suggests that you see the nation state as a vehicle for advancing the goals of classical liberalism.

I also hear in your words echoes of Ernest Renan, who, in his influential 1882 lecture 'What Is a Nation?' saw the nation as a vehicle for realizing liberty. Renan, too, was critical of attempts to define a nation by race, language or religion, recognizing these as inadequate foundations. Instead, he argued that a nation is built on an inclusive and shared sense of the past—on a rich legacy of collective memories, shaped as much by what is remembered as by what is forgotten. A nation is fed by a people's desire to live together, to continue to invest in the heritage that they've jointly received. For Renan, a nation's existence is not fixed but renewed daily through the will of its people, much like an individual's affirmation of life. He also warned against coercive nationalism, adding that 'a nation never has a true interest in annexing or holding territory that does not wish to be annexed or held'.

Please correct me if I'm wrong. What I hear you saying is that nationalism is not a Western idea that was imposed on the non-West. You see it as a natural outgrowth of a kind of historical change that happened to have begun in the West and then caught on as modernity spread. The nation state is an aspect of modernity and its forms of knowledge and self-awareness. And the idea of nationalism that you subscribe to, and hope for, is one that helps achieve the goals of classical liberalism, in which equal citizenship, democracy, and basic freedoms and rights for all are at the very heart of the nation state and ensuring which requires that it be a secular nationalism. In fact, that's how you define nationalism, and you regard any departures from it as a corrupted form—not true nationalism.

That is a bracing view. In real life, however, nationalism the world over is prone to the same kinds of illiberal tendencies, risks, idolatry, obsessions and passions that religion also tends to foster in people, and which can destroy a society, or at least stifle its human potential. Some nationalisms go bonkers with religio-ethnic identitarians. Think Zionism and Hindutva. But even when it doesn't, nationalism still makes up offenses such as sedition and labels like 'anti-national', arguably akin to the offenses of blasphemy and apostasy in some religions. It entertains talk of martyrdom. With 'Bharat Mata', the nation even takes on the trappings of a deity. As in organized religions, nationalisms tend to evoke deep primal passions around a powerful fictional entity at its core—'the nation'.

Consequently, 'supporting the nation' begins to be equated with defending its jingoism and any ethical questioning of that stance is seen as betrayal. Such nationalist passions, in their intensity and blindness, have counterparts in organized religions. Some nationalists are even willing to sacrifice their lives for the supposed defence of their nation—many speak of it as a revered, 'supreme sacrifice'. And all this surfaces especially during conflict with other nations, as we see between India and Pakistan, which our political elites cynically exploit for their own partisan gains.

I suppose all one can hope for, and work towards—as we do with religion—is a nationalism that is inclusive enough and *relatively* benign. The results vary of course, as we see in the world today.

ROMILA: One can always hope nationalism takes a positive form, but there are no guarantees. Every society has been through various forms, some carrying the potential for constructive outcomes, and others so steeped in negative elements that the positive barely surfaced. I have seen enough of human ambition to know that not everything will turn out for the best. But if the outcome is reasonably good, one carries on with it and tries to make it better. Nationalism is characterized by not being static, and it can be adjusted to new requirements, while still retaining its core principles. When its actions cease to honour those principles, they can—and should—be questioned and opposed.

Please don't get me wrong. I am not being negative; I am keeping over-positivism in control. If there is one thing I have learnt from my long life, it is that nothing, however good, will last forever. There are periods when things work well and others when they don't. One has to accept the constant change. And ultimately, it's also a question of how one chooses to live one's life. Today another thought of the *longue durée* could well become a nightmare if we mishandle things like AI and climate change. Will they hasten the demise of nations and nationalism and infuse our world with some other system?

A Madhubani painting showing Krishna with gopis, by Sharwan Paswan. Source: Lalit Kala Akademy

23

Some Favourite Creative Works from Early India

NAMIT: Okay, now a fun question about literature. Your first degree in college was in literature and I understand that you remain keenly interested in the subject.

ROMILA: Yes.

NAMIT: The love of literature, I personally think, is very conducive to historical sense! And we Indians have inherited a large corpus of creative works of the imagination from early India, spanning the spiritual, the literary and the philosophical. I've often marvelled at Macaulay's chutzpah when he claimed that 'A single shelf of a good European library was worth the whole native literature of India and Arabia' (laughs).

I would love to hear about some of your favourite works from ancient and early medieval India, which has been the primary focus of your scholarship. I have in mind here texts and authors, to name a few, like the Upanishads, the *Dhammapada* and other early Buddhist texts, remnants of the *Brhaspati Sutra* of the Charvakas, the two great epics including the Gita, Sangam literature, the *Kural*, Panini, Patanjali, the *Arthashastra*, the *Therigatha*, *Milind Panha*, the Puranas, Ashvaghosha, Hala's *Gaha Sattasai*, Nagarjuna, the *Kama Sutra*, Kalidasa, Aryabhata, Sudraka's *Mrchchakatikam*, Bhartrhari, Dignaga and other thinkers of Nalanda, Vishakhadatta, Banabhatta, Dandin, Bhavabhuti and many others. What are some texts from ancient and early medieval India whose inner qualities you've admired the most? Notice that I've purposely left out the Manu-smriti!

ROMILA: My list is possibly peculiar to me. For example, out of all the Vedic texts, the one that speaks to me most closely, is the Katha Upanishad, which is a dialogue between a youth called Nachiketas and Yama, the god of death. And it's on immortality, knowledge, the self, liberation and suchlike. It has appealed to me enormously because I'm intrigued by the obsession that we humans have with the question of immortality. Being so mortal, immortality is absolutely the other end of the spectrum, so we're reaching out to it all the time. It is fascinating how dominant that idea has been. And I found that in this Upanishad, the idea of somebody talking to death and questioning death, and death responding, was intellectually really smart and emotionally moving. The idea was also great fun. And I had at one time, in my foolishness, thought that I might do a contemporary translation of it. But then I realized that a meaningful translation would be beyond me, as it requires much greater sensitivity to the philosophical ideas of that time—and perhaps even now! It raises questions, some stunning, some fun, that are complicated, and I did not wish to attempt simplifying them.

Anyway, so that was one text. Among literary works, I love the plays of Bhasa (first–second century CE). They are about what happens to all of us, that which we face, do, act upon and so on. There's an underlying humour to the plays, which I found most attractive, although they're not comic. There's something to be said for that.

I greatly enjoyed reading the *Harshacharita* (c. 640 CE) of Banabhatta, or Bana, which I have had to do a few times as I have written on it. It's possibly one of the best biographies I've ever read, partly because Bana as the author is both present and he's there, and sometimes he's not really there. For instance, the way he decides that he will actually write the biography is slightly complicated. The king invites him to write it after a careful assessment, and Bana agrees but with some hesitation. There's a certain play on dissidence. His comments on the royal family are perceptive. He quotes even some disparaging remarks from the villagers when the army is on the move. He is a highly intelligent observer. I found that really so good because the biography expands from being just about the king and the court into something bigger. It tells us more about the life of people. I liked that very much.

Of course, before all of this, my great obsession was with the Ashokan inscriptions, on which I wrote my PhD, and which I think are really quite remarkable. H.G. Wells did sum him up as a remarkable ruler, but I think what is deeply impressive about him is that he's not just a ruler, he's a human being who is conscious of being both a ruler and what we would today call a citizen and an ordinary human being. There was indeed something extraordinary about this man. Every time I read the edicts, I get fresh pleasure and a little more understanding perhaps of the world we live in.

The other text that I always read for wisdom and some fun is Kalhana's history of Kashmir, the *Rajatarangini* (twelfth century). It goes all over the place and addresses many topics. It reads rather like a medieval novel. He has rational arguments, and he has irrational arguments, and the reader is either battling with him or agreeing with him. I enjoyed that enormously.

Those, I would say, are some of my favourite texts.

NAMIT: Oh, that was most enjoyable to hear. Thank you for this marvellous reflection.

Painted house of the Kabui (or Rongmeis) Naga tribe of Manipur.
Display at Museum of Man, Bhopal.
Photo: Namit Arora.

24

On Changing Our Own Interpretations

NAMIT: Earlier in our conversation, you spoke about the historical method. Now, a scholar's commitment to the historical method also implies that she's committed to revising her earlier interpretations, if better arguments or evidence turn up. Can you think of any historical interpretations on which you've substantially changed your mind?

ROMILA: Well, there is one that got me into a prolonged argument. I mean, there were others too, smaller ones, but this was bigger. When I originally wrote my thesis on the Mauryas, on Ashoka—almost seventy years ago—I followed the standard view of the time: that empires were vast territories ruled by a single, highly centralized administration, with all decisions flowing directly from the imperial centre. But over the years, I began to question this picture. After all, the Mauryan territory was extensive, almost the entire subcontinent. Could such enormous territories be governed in a centralized manner, especially in that era, with its limited means of contact, communication and administration?

I began to think differently. Finally, I think in 1987—thirty years after my thesis—I gave a couple of lectures in Calcutta titled 'The Mauryas Revisited'. One of them asked whether we should continue to view empires as highly centralized organizations. I questioned that assumption. Empires, I argued, do not come together all at once but piece by piece. Each newly conquered territory requires the establishment of some form of administration, and additional regions are added incrementally. I now saw the Mauryan empire as beginning with the Ganges Plain, the first area brought under Mauryan control. It had a certain amount of unity, owing to kingdoms that had been around in that area. I called that the 'metropolitan state'—the part of the empire that could be governed directly as a centralized system.

At a different level, in the outlying or frontier zones that gradually came into the empire, were what I called 'core areas', such as Gandhara. These were governed with some degree of decentralization because they were far away and difficult to reach. And on the break-up of the empire, they tended to become independent states. Other core areas, for instance, were in Gujarat and Odisha. Their administration was inspired by the centralized model of administration but was more decentralized. After all, if a letter from Pataliputra (Patna) took two months to reach Gujarat, decisions could not always wait for its arrival. There would have to be some decentralized decision-making, which made these regions functionally distinct from the imperial centre.

The third category I introduced was regions without direct administrative control, such as those inhabited largely by adivasis—the forest dwellers Ashoka mentioned in his inscriptions. These groups were not taxed in a formal sense, nor were their lives regulated much. Instead, they supplied forest produce to the officers of the administration. I called these the 'peripheral areas'—semi-autonomous, largely forested regions. The *Arthashastra*, for example, says that these people have to be told to bring whatever forest produce they have agreed to supply to officials of the state. They were not permitted to break away and be on their own, but neither were they subject to close or absolute control. They seem to have been semi-autonomous.

I argued therefore that imperial systems could be understood as comprising a metropolitan state, the core areas and the peripheral areas. And I put this out as a thesis. The reactions were mixed. Some Indian historians were strongly critical, insisting that all empires are necessarily centralized, and that by questioning this foundational tenet I was undermining the very concept of empire. They objected to my suggestion of smaller administrative units or even superficial forms of governance, which, in their view, did not align with the idea of empire. Other historians, however, showed interest in the categories I had introduced. Two years later, there was a big conference on imperial systems at the Institute of Historical Research at London University. They invited me to present my thesis at the plenary, as my ideas had gathered some attention. My paper provoked lively discussion, particularly around the central question it raised: Can empires be understood as operating through two or three distinct modes of administration rather than through a single, uniform system? And I was struck by how historians of Europe engaged seriously with my suggestion, discussing it across several sessions of the conference—something many prominent Indian historians had earlier dismissed without debate. However, it has now become part of the inquiry into the administration of the empire among some Indian historians as well. The critiques it attracted did not lead me to revise my interpretation; on the contrary, I found a couple of the more publicized objections quite untenable. If anything, I'm even more convinced that patterns of imperial administration in early times need to be researched more fully.

So that was one case where I did rethink my ideas. And I still stay with the second idea. I don't regard imperial systems as altogether uniformly centralized.

NAMIT: That's a good example. Do any others come to mind?

ROMILA: Not at the moment. This attempt at rethinking on my part, I had hoped would focus on patterns of imperial administrations and if they differed then how and why they did so and what were the consequences. I think such a comparative analysis of even just the Indian subcontinent would be worth doing. There are patterns in administration that differ over region and time. I was hoping that someone would suggest a conference on patterns of administration that encourage imperial systems or discourage them and how they differed. But this did not happen. However, my lecture raised some strange reactions in India. I was accused of saying that there was a ritual relationship between the administration and the local people. But a ritual relationship didn't come into the picture and that was not what I had referred to. I was speaking of degrees and types of administration. And I think it is true of India even today—some areas are much more centrally controlled and governed in a particular way, and other areas are much more decentralized, inevitably. Of course, with improved communication and other changes in systems of government, the pattern of administration does change. Another attempted critique argued that an immense advance in trade accounted for the decentralization, but this did not result in the categories I had suggested. This argument however does not hold, as the substantial change in trade dates to the later, post-Mauryan period.

Nevertheless, there seems to be an inability to accept flexibility and diversity in human relations. For some, it's got to be in a particular mould. Yet, an essential necessity of historical research is precisely to encourage the asking of questions, especially of existing knowledge, so that if the advancing of knowledge on that theme is required, it can be done. The caveat is that the advancing has to be based on proven evidence and causality deriving from rational and logical connections. That leads to historical research providing new information, new forms of analyses and a fresh understanding of what is being researched.

NAMIT: I sure hope more historians take your approach more often in rethinking their prior ideas and interpretations.

ROMILA: One can only talk about it and leave it at that.

NAMIT: Indeed. Well, believe it or not, that's all the questions I have! We have covered quite a range of topics too. Thank you for sitting down with me. Do you have any closing thoughts for this conversation?

ROMILA: We have spoken about many aspects of history, and I hope that some of these themes will be taken up by other historians and discussed further. As I always say, all existing knowledge has to be questioned if we want to gain further knowledge.

NAMIT: I couldn't agree more. Prof. Thapar, this has been an immense honour, a pleasure and a great learning experience for me. Thank you so much!

Acknowledgements

By Namit Arora and Romila Thapar

The idea of such a conversation was sparked at a fortuitous meeting between us in March 2024. By the time we got going, its scope had grown, eventually becoming a book that we hoped would speak to both general readers and students of history.

Once we had a draft manuscript, we turned to a circle of friends and colleagues for their impressions, including six professional historians and six generalists. We are grateful to the following individuals (in no particular order) for their generosity of time and spirit, and their thoughtful and at times rather blunt feedback: Meera Visvanathan, Ann Ninan, Megha Malhotra, Mohan Rao, Usha Alexander, Vijay Poduri, Kesavan Veluthat, Ranabir Chakravarti, Krishna Kumar, Aloka Parasher Sen, Neeladri Bhattacharya and Nalini Taneja. Whether in untangling a knotty passage, flagging a blind spot or an oversight, disagreeing with something, suggesting further arguments or improvements in structure or tone, or simply cheering us on, we thank each of them warmly. Their comments refined our thinking, sharpened our engagement with the topics at hand, and enriched the flow and substance of the dialogue. This book is stronger for their quiet yet vital contributions. And how does one even begin to thank the stars that aligned to bring the two of us together for this project?

Our thanks also go to Kanishka Gupta and his literary agency for diligently working behind the scenes to resolve this book's path to publication. We appreciate the editorial team at Penguin Random House India, including Manasi Subramaniam and Manali Das, for their insightful feedback, diligent editing and coordination of the cover design led by Aakriti Khurana, as well as the legal reviews by the team at Obhan & Associates. We are also indebted to Asad Zaidi and Nalini Taneja, editors at Three Essays Collective, for their resourcefulness and dedication in ensuring the book's publication in international markets. We are grateful to Mitchell Abdul Karim Crites for letting us use several images of art from his collection.

May this book find the audience it deserves!

Endnotes

1 See 'Fatty residues on ancient pottery reveal meat-heavy diets of Indus Civilization' by University of Cambridge, phys.org, 9 December 2020.

2 During his highly charged Rath Yatra (1990) from Somanatha to Ayodhya, L.K. Advani explicitly invoked the memory of Somanatha to fuel the agitation to build a temple at the site of the Babri Masjid. A recent example of this sentiment occurs in an article by Rakesh Krishnan Simha, 'One Thousand Years of Iconoclasm: The Beast that Demolished Somnath Continues to Haunt India' in Stop Hindudvesha, an initiative of the Vishwa Hindu Parishad of America, 18 Dec 2024 (see 'closing remarks').

3 These views are rather well-documented in the seminal texts of Hindu nationalism and have been analysed by scholars. See Marzia Casolari's 'Hindutva's Foreign Tie-up in the 1930s: Archival Evidence', *Economic and Political Weekly*, January 22, 2000, pp: 218–228 (full PDF is online at https://www.sacw.net/DC/CommunalismCollection/ArticlesArchive/casolari.pdf) and articles on sites such as the Caravan (https://caravanmagazine.in/history/rss-golwalkar-links-nazism), Forsea (https://forsea.co/how-fascism-nazism-influenced-hindu-nationalism/) and NewsClick (https://www.newsclick.in/why-jaitley-needs-study-link-between-rss-and-fascism).

4 See for instance Ashis Nandy's *The Intimate Enemy: Loss and Recovery of Self Under Colonialism*, Partha Chatterjee's *The Nation and Its*

Fragments: Colonial and Postcolonial Histories, and Christophe Jaffrelot's *Religion, Caste, and Politics in India*.

5 See 'Shashi Tharoor Vs Vikram Sampath: Debating Heritage, History & Hubris | India Today Conclave 2021', https://www.youtube.com/watch?v=LZS7dL0QaX8 (Sampath amplifies these claims between 32:30–33:10).

6 These changes have been analysed in the media by many authors. See: Suhasini Raj, 'New Indian Textbooks Purged of Muslim History and Hindu Extremism', *New York Times*, 6 April 2023; Nandini Singh, 'Harappan civilisation gets a new identity in NCERT's new class 6 textbook', *Business Standard*, 22 July 2024; K. Kannan, 'History as battlefield — the perils of reversing the past', *The Hindu*, 15 April 2025 and Ruchika Sharma, 'Mughals in NCERT Class VIII textbook: An inaccurate retelling with a communal twist', *Indian Express*, 17 July 2025.

7 See, for instance, the 2021 calendar (https://www.shunya.net/Text/Misc/IKS_Calendar2021.pdf) produced by the Centre of Excellence for Indian Knowledge Systems at IIT Kharagpur, which was critiqued by multiple media outlets, including Raiot (https://raiot.in/on-the-indian-knowledge-systems-calendar-from-whatsapp-department-of-iit-kharagpur/) and twice in The Wire: C.P. Rajendra, 'How a Calendar Exposed the Falling Standards of an IIT', Wire, 2 January 2024; Rahul Siddharthan, 'The IIT Kharagpur Calendar Is the Right's Attempt To Appropriate the Indus Valley Civilisation', Wire, 29 December 2021.

8 Some articles that document this fear have appeared in Maya Prabhu, 'Is free speech under threat in Modi's India?', Al Jazeera, 3 August 2027; Harsh Bora, 'Where the Mind Is . . . Full of Fear', *India Today*, 18 November 2019 and Meenakshi Ganguly, 'In India, Speaking Out on Abuses Carries a High Price', Human Rights Watch, 12 November 2021.

9 Visvanathan, Meera, 'Against History: Sanjeev Sanyal's attempts to rewrite India's past', *The Caravan*, 30 September 2021

10 Sanyal makes the Rig Veda claim in *The Indian Renaissance: India's Rise After a Thousand Years of Decline*. The Bhimbetka claim appears in *The Ocean of Churn: How the Indian Ocean Shaped Human History*.

11 Scroll staff, '85% of Indians support autocracy or military rule, shows Pew survey', Scroll.in, 14 March 2024

12 Razib Khan, 'West Asian ancestry in South Asian Muslims', Brown-Pundits.com, 7 March 2021

13 Anthony, David W., *The Horse, the Wheel, and Language: How Bronze-Age Riders from the Eurasian Steppes Shaped the Modern World*, Princeton University Press, 2007, Chapter 15.

14 Another example comes from the site of Newgrange in Ireland, where the Bell Beaker people, also of Steppe descent, were associated with horse sacrifices related to kingship rituals. See 'The Origins of Domestic Horses in North-west Europe: new Direct Dates on the Horses of Newgrange, Ireland', *Proceedings of the Prehistoric Society* 79, 2013, pp. 91–103.

15 Three volumes that study early Indo-European societies and their commonalities include Kristiansen, K., Kroonen, G., & Willerslev, E. (Eds.), *The Indo-European Puzzle Revisited: Integrating Archaeology, Genetics, and Linguistics*. Cambridge University Press, 2023; Olsen, Birgit Anette (Editor), *Tracing the Indo-Europeans: New evidence from archaeology and historical linguistics*, Oxbow Books, 2019, and Kuz'mina, Elena E., *The Origin of the Indo-Iranians*, Brill, 2007.

16 Dhere, R.C., Feldhaus, Anne (translator), *The Rise of a Folk God: Vitthal of Pandharpur*, Oxford University Press, 2011. First published in Marathi as *Shree Vitthal: Ek Mahasamanvay*, Padmagandha Prakashan, 1984.

17 Dutta, Amartya Kumar, 'Aryabhata and Axial Rotation of Earth', *Resonance*, Vol.11, No.4, pp. 56–74, 2006.

18 Mukhia, Harbans, *The Mughals of India*, Blackwell Publishing, 2004, pp. 146.

19 A. Basu, N. Sarkar-Roy, & P.P. Majumder, Genomic reconstruction of the history of extant populations of India reveals five distinct ancestral components and a complex structure, Proc. Natl. Acad. Sci. U.S.A. 113 (6) 1594-1599, https://doi.org/10.1073/pnas.1513197113 (2016).

20 Eaton, Richard, *Indian in the Persianate Age: 1000-1765*, University of California Press, 2019, pp. 388.

Select Bibliography

Ali, Daud, *Courtly Culture and Political Life in Early Medieval India*, Cambridge, 2004

Allchin, F.R., Bridget Allchin, Robin Conningham, George Erdosy and Dilip K. Chakrabarti, *The Archaeology of Early Historic South Asia: The Emergence of Cities and States*, University of Cambridge, 1995

Alpers, Edward A., *The Indian Ocean in World History*, Oxford University Press, 2014

Ambedkar, B.R., *The Annihilation of Caste*, 1936

Amrith, Sunil, *The Burning Earth: A History*, WW Norton and Company, 2024

Anderson, Benedict, *Imagined Communities: Reflections on the Origin and Spread of Nationalism*, Verso, 1983

Anthony, David W, *The Horse, the Wheel, and Language: How Bronze-Age Riders from the Eurasian Steppes Shaped the Modern World*, Princeton University Press, 2010

Arora, Namit, *Indians: A Brief History of a Civilization*, Penguin India, 2021

--, *The Lottery of Birth: On Inherited Social Inequalities*, Three Essays Collective, 2017

Asher, Catherine B., and Cynthia Talbot, *India before Europe*, Cambridge University Press, 2006

Basham, A.L., *History and Doctrine of the Ajivikas: A Vanished Indian Sect*, London: Luzac 1951 (Motilal Banarasidass, Indian reprint, 2002)

-- (Ed), *A Cultural History of India*, Oxford University Press, 1975

Bhargava, Meena, and Pratyay Nath (Eds), *The Early Modern in South Asia: Querying Modernity, Periodization, and History*, Cambridge University Press, 2022

Bhattacharya, Neeladri, *The Great Agrarian Conquest: The Colonial Reshaping of a Rural World*, Permanent Black, 2019

Bosworth, C.E., *The Ghaznavids: Their Empire in Afghanistan and Eastern India 994–1040*, Edinburgh University Press, 1963

Bronkhurst, Johannes, *How the Brahmins Won: From Alexander to the Guptas*, Brill, 2016

Chakrabarti, Kunal, and Kanad Sinha (Eds), *State, Power and Legitimacy: The Gupta Kingdom*, Primus Books, 2019

Chakravarti, Ranabir, *Trade and Traders in Early Indian Society*, Manohar (third edition) 2020

--, *The Pull Towards the Coast and Other Essays: The Indian Ocean History and the Subcontinent before 1500 CE*, Primus Books, 2020

Chakravarti, Uma, *Gendering Caste: Through a Feminist Lens*, SAGE Publications Pvt. Ltd, 2018

Chamapakalakshmi, R., Trade, *Ideology and Urbanization: South India 300 BC to AD 1300*, Oxford University Press, 1996

Chattopadhyaya, Brajadulal, *The Making of Early Medieval India*, Oxford University Press 1994 (second edition 2012)

--, *Representing the Other? Sanskrit Sources and the Muslims, Eighth to Thirteenth Century*, Manohar, 1998

--, *The Concept of Bharatavarsha and Other Essays*, Permanent Black, 2017

Chattopadhyaya, Debiprasad, *Science and Philosophy in Ancient India*, Aakar Books, 2013

K.N. Chaudhuri, *Trade and Civilisation in the Indian Ocean: An Economic History from the Rise of Islam to 1750*, Cambridge University Press, 1985

--, *Asia before Europe, Economy and Civilisation of the Indian Ocean from the Rise of Islam to 1750*, Cambridge University Press, 1990

Das Gupta, Ashin, compiled by Uma Dasgupta, *The World of the Indian Ocean Merchant, 1500–1800: Collected Essays*, Oxford University Press, 2001

Das Gupta Ashin and M.N. Pearson (Eds), *India and the Indian Ocean 1500–1800*, Oxford University Press, 1985

Desai, Devangana, *Erotic Sculpture of India: Socio-Cultural Study*, Munshiram Manoharlal Publishers, 1974, reprinted 1985

Diamond, Jared, *Guns, Germs, and Steel: The Fates of Human Societies*, WW Norton, 1997

Doniger, Wendy; *The Hindus: An Alternative History*; Penguin, 2009

Dumont, Louis, *Homo Hierarchicus*, University of Chicago Press; Second edition, 1981

Eaton, Richard M., *India in the Persianate Age: 1000–1765*, Allen Lane, 2019

--, *A Social History of the Deccan, 1300-1761: Eight Indian Lives*, Cambridge University Press, 2005

--, *Temple Desecration and Indo-Muslim States*; Journal of Islamic Studies 11:3 (2000), pp. 283–319, Oxford Centre for Islamic Studies 2000

Elverskog, Johan, *Buddhism and Islam on the Silk Road*, University of Pennsylvania Press, 2011

Fogelin, Lars, *An Archaeological History of Indian Buddhism*, Oxford University Press, 2015

Foucault, Michel, and Paul Rabinow (Ed), *The Foucault Reader*, Pantheon, 1984

Ganeri, Jonardon (Ed), *The Oxford Handbook of Indian Philosophy*, Oxford University Press, 2017

Habib, Irfan, *The Agrarian System of Mughal India 1556–1707*, Oxford University Press, 1963; revised edition, 1999

Harari, Yuval Noah, *Sapiens: A Brief History of Humankind*, Vintage, 2015

Hobsbawm, E.J., *Nations and Nationalism since 1780*, Cambridge University Press, 1992

Jaffrelot, Christophe, *Religion, Caste and Politics in India*, Primus Books, 2010

Jha, D.N., *The Myth of the Holy Cow*, Navayana, 2010

Jodhka, S.S., *Caste in Contemporary India*, Routledge (second edition), 2017

Karashima, Noburu (Ed), *A Concise History of South India: Issues and Interpretations*, Oxford University Press, 2014

Karve, Iravati, *Yuganta: The End of an Epoch* (English translation from Marathi by W. Norman Brown, Orient Longman (reprint), 2006

Joseph, Tony, *Early Indians: The Story of Our Ancestors and Where We Came From*, Juggernaut, 2018

Keay, John, *India: A History*, HarperCollins, 2000

Kuhn, Thomas S., *The Structure of Scientific Revolutions*, University of Chicago Press, 1962

Kumar, Sunil, *Demolishing Myths or Mosques and Temples? Readings on History and Temple Desecration in Medieval India*, Three Essays Collective, 2008

Hermann, Kulke, and Bhairavi Prasad Sahu (Ed), *The Routledge Handbook of the State in Premodern India*, Routledge, 2022

Lal, Pranay, *Indica: A Deep Natural History of the Indian Subcontinent*, Penguin India, 2016

Miller, Barbara Stoller (Ed), *Powers of Art: Patronage in Indian Culture*, Oxford University Press, 1998

Mohan, Peggy, *Wanderers, Kings, Merchants: The Story of India through Its Languages*, Penguin India 2021

Mukhia, Harbans, *The Mughals of India*, John Wiley & Sons, 2004

Mukul, Akshaya, *Gita Press and the Making of Hindu India*, Harper Collins India, 2015

Nagaraj, D.N., *The Flaming Feet and Other Essays: The Dalit Movement in India*, Permanent Black, 2011

Nanda, Meera, *Science in Saffron: Skeptical Essays on History of Science*, Three Essays Collective, 2016

Olivelle, Patrick and M. McClish (Eds), *The Arthaśāstra: Selections from the Classic Indian Work on Statecraft*, Hackett Publishing, 2012

Omvedt, Gail, *Buddhism in India: Challenging Brahmanism and Caste*, SAGE Publications Pvt. Ltd, 2003

Panikkar, K.N., *Culture, Ideology, Hegemony: Intellectuals and Social Consciousness in Colonial India*, Anthem, 2002

Parashar, Aloka, *The Mlecchas in Early India: A Study in Attitudes towards Outsiders in India up to AD 600*, Munshiram Manoharlal, 1991

--, *Gender, Religion and Local History: The Early Deccan*, Primus Books, 2023

Parpola, Asko, *The Roots of Hinduism: The Early Aryans and the Indus Civilization*, Oxford University Press, 2015

Pechilis, Karen (Ed.), *A Cultural History of Hinduism in the Post-Classical Age*, Bloomsbury Academic, 2024

Reich, David, *Who We Are and How We Got Here: Ancient DNA and the New Science of the Human Past*, Oxford University Press, 2018

Ratnagar, Shereen, *Understanding Harappa: Civilization in the Greater Indus Valley*, Tulika, 2006

--, *Being Tribal*, Primus Books, 2019

Rawls, John, *A Theory of Justice*, Harvard University Press, 1971

Rege, Sharmila, *Sociology of Gender: The Challenge of Feminist Sociological Thought*, SAGE India, 2003

Roy, Kumkum, *The Power of Gender and the Gender of Power: Explorations in Early Indian History*, Oxford University Press, 2010

-- (Ed.), *Women in Early Indian Societies*, Manohar, 1999

Roy, Tirthankar, *An Economic History of India 1707–1857*, Routledge, 2021

Said, Edward W., *Orientalism: Western Conceptions of the Orient*, Vintage, 1978

Sandel, Michael, *Justice: What's the Right Thing to Do?* Farrar, Straus and Giroux, 2009

Sarkar, Sumit, *Modern India 1885–1947*, McMillan, 1985

Sarkar, Sumit, and Sarkar, Tanika (Eds), *Caste in Modern India*, 2 vol, Permanent Black, 2013

Satia, Priya, *Time's Monster: History, Conscience and Britain's Empire*, Allen Lane, 2020

Singh, Upinder, *Ancient India: Culture of Contradictions*, Aleph Book Company, 2021

--, *Political Violence in Ancient India*, Harvard University Press, 2017

Sinha, Kanad, *From Dasarajna to Kurukshetra: Making of a Historical Tradition*, Oxford University Press, 2021

Sharma, R.S., *India's Ancient Past*, Oxford University Press, 2005

Subbarayalu, Y., *South India under the Cholas*, Oxford University Press, 2011

Subramanian, Ajantha, *The Caste of Merit: Engineering Education in India*, Harvard University Press, 2019

Teltumbde, Anand, *The Persistence of Caste: The Khairlanji Murders & India's Hidden Apartheid*, Navayana, 2010

Thapar, Romila, *Aśoka and the Decline of the Mauryas*, 1961 (revised 1998); Oxford University Press

--, *The Penguin History of Early India: From the Origins to AD 1300*, Penguin, 2003

--, *Somanatha: The Many Voices of a History*; Verso. 2005

--, *The Past Before Us: Historical Traditions of Early North India*; HUP, 2013

--, *The Past as Present*, Aleph Book Company, 2014

Thapar, Romila, A.G. Noorani and Sadanand Menon, *On Nationalism*, Aleph Book Company, 2016

Thapar, Romila, Michael Witzel, Jaya Menon, Kai Friese and Razib Khan, *Which of Us Are Aryans?* Aleph Book Company, 2019

Thapar, Romila, Ramin Jahanbegloo, Neeladri Bhattacharya, *Talking History: Romila Thapar in conversation with Ramin Jahanbegloo, with the participation of Neeladri Bhattacharya*; Aleph Book Company, 2017

Truschke, Audrey, *The Language of History: Sanskrit Narratives of Muslim Pasts*, Allen Lane, 2021

Valmiki, Omprakash, and Arun Prabha Mukherjee (Trans.), *Joothan: A Dalit's Life*, Columbia University Press, 2008

Veluthat, Kesavan, *The Political Structure in Early Medieval South India*, Orient Blackswan, 1994

Westerhoff, Jan, *Nāgārjuna's Madhyamaka: A Philosophical Introduction*, Oxford University Press, 2009

Xaxa, Abhay F., and D.N. Devy, *Being Adivasi: Existence, Entitlements: Existence, Entitlements, Exclusion*, Vintage, 2021

Index

About the Authors

About Romila Thapar

Romila Thapar was born in 1931 into a Punjabi Khatri family with a home in Lahore. Her father was a medical doctor in the British army, and his job took him and his family across undivided India. She spent her early years in places like the Thal Fort in the Frontier Province, Peshawar, Rawalpindi, Dalhousie, and, from age eleven, in Pune. The languages she learnt in her youth were English, Punjabi, Hindi and Urdu, with Sanskrit later in college.

In the north-west, her father's circle of friends had included Khan Abdul Ghaffar Khan. In Pune, when Gandhi was fasting in 1943, her father's friends provided him medical care. Still a schoolgirl, she attended Gandhi's prayer meetings and gathered up courage to ask for his autograph. He obliged but urged her to abandon the silk she wore for the occasion and switch to khadi, which she dutifully did for a while. She also met Nehru later as part of a college group. Both Gandhi and Nehru became her heroes in her youth.

In her mid-teens, visiting her older brother, a journalist in Bombay, she met many free-thinking young liberals and leftist nationalists. At fifteen, nearing August 1947, she reflected on the meaning of independence and what it means to be 'Indian', engaging in school debates on the kind of society Indians should try to build as a free people.

During her undergraduate years, she switched colleges—and subjects, eventually settling on history. Like many at that age, she too wrote poetry that, she now confesses, makes her shudder. She loved swimming, horse riding, playing hockey, and participating in intercollegiate debates and drama competitions, 'usually bringing home the trophy'. She pursued films and literature from around the world.

Among the books that made a strong impression on her was Simone de Beauvoir's *The Second Sex*. In her words, it 'brought many social attitudes, even of Indian society, into focus' and made her 'far more sensitive to the issues raised by feminist writers in later decades', though, she has written, 'it did not turn me into a feminist . . . my awareness of feminism came to me rather late!'

Thapar was eager to study in England, so her father gave her a choice. He had saved enough for her dowry; she could use the money either for that purpose or to fund two years of education abroad. This was a no-brainer to her. She initially set her sights on Oxford but failed its entrance exam (decades later, in 1997, Oxford would award her an honorary doctorate, a moment of sweet vindication). The University of London's School of Oriental and African Studies (SOAS) accepted her to study history but required her to clear the History Hons. BA degree. Over the next two years, she earned an accelerated second bachelor's degree at SOAS, learning history from resident scholars like A.L. Basham, and others such as Eric Hobsbawm, Arnaldo Momigliano and some visiting ones, such as D.D. Kosambi. By the end of those two years, her funds ran out, and her parents began calling her home to find her a suitable boy.

Thapar agonized about her way forward. She loved being in London, but she needed a job to stay on, which wasn't easy. Impressed by her potential, Basham urged her to apply for a PhD and a research fellowship in history. Being an academic hadn't interested her much, but she had few alternatives, so she applied for it. After a gruelling interview, she secured the fellowship. This was roughly the moment, she says, when she committed to becoming a historian. In 1958, at twenty-seven, she finished her PhD under Basham's guidance with an influential dissertation titled *Ashoka and the Decline of the Mauryas*.

She taught for a year at SOAS and returned to India in 1961 to take up teaching roles—first at Kurukshetra University and, in 1963, at Delhi University. In her political orientation, she saw herself as 'left-of-centre', but not a political Marxist. She disliked Stalinism. Her interest in Marxism was mainly as a materialist philosophy of history and its ability to offer on occasion compelling explanations of historical processes. The *Annales* School and Max Weber also interested her in their approaches to the past.

In 1970, at age thirty-nine, Thapar joined the newly minted Jawaharlal Nehru University (JNU) in Delhi, which began the most intellectually exciting phase of her career, and where she did some of her most important work. As one of the founders of the Centre for Historical Studies at JNU, she helped shape what would become perhaps the world's leading research institute for Indian history. Reflecting on her time there, she recalls how 'democratic and liberal discussions were regarded as essential to shaping thoughtful individuals'. Unfortunately, things have declined significantly in recent years. JNU's current administrators, she has written, 'confuse a university with a *pathashala* [traditional village school]' and discourage 'questions and debates as part of the normal activities of a university.'

As is now standard among historians worldwide, Thapar supports a secular and rational approach to advancing historical knowledge, grounded in interdisciplinary methods. She acknowledges that imaginative retellings of the past—whether in fiction, folklore or films—will always exist but insists that such narratives must not be conflated with history, which rests on empirical evidence and reasoned argument. Over time, she has increasingly blended cultural and material history in her work, while also contributing to feminist and Dalit historiography, evident in her monograph on the multiple narratives of Shakuntala and her lecture on the very idea of civilization.

Thapar went on to become a preeminent historian of early India. She has authored over twenty-five books, including *The Penguin History of Early India: From the Origins to AD 1300* (2003). Many leading global institutions have recognized her with awards and honorary doctorates, including the Kluge Prize, which is awarded by the US Library of Congress for lifetime achievement in the study of humanity, widely considered on par with the Nobel Prize in fields not covered by the latter.

Thapar has taken active interest in public life and supports many social causes—including the cause of credible historical writing in India, which has long put her and many other academic historians of India in the crosshairs of those who seek to replace evidence-based history with an ethnocentric narrative of a glorified past. She is also well known for her efforts to make history more accessible and relevant to a broader audience. In the '70s and '80s, she played a significant role in shaping the history curriculum of NCERT textbooks for schools. She has often engaged in public debates through the media and other non-academic platforms to help foster a more informed and reflective civic discourse.

About Namit Arora

Namit Arora was raised in Gwalior, where his father worked as a textile engineer and his mother managed the home. An unwavering nastika since thirteen, he would later acquire an abiding secular interest in the varieties of religious experience. Like most middle-class kids of his day, he too was herded towards vocations deemed 'safer': engineering and medicine. History, badly taught and undervalued, barely caught his interest back then. At twenty-one, after a BTech from the Indian Institute of Technology Kharagpur (1989), he left for graduate school in the US. Living abroad raised for him deeper questions of culture, history and identity, pushing him to understand his country and his place in the world better.

His tech career in Silicon Valley, from its start in the early 1990s, felt intellectually and spiritually vacant. His seriocomic way of relating to this subculture's vanities and pretensions later led him to write a novel set in that milieu. His cultivated detachment from it freed him up to explore other interests in parallel: reading, writing, travel, photography, dating women, learning Spanish, visiting India annually and more. He began a self-directed education in the humanities and social sciences, focusing more on literature, philosophy and history. He took courses of dubious practical value at Stanford and spent weekends holed up in its Green Library, immersed in reading books and writing essays on topics ranging from classical Greek historians to early Islam (archived on his website shunya.net).

Namit has, since boyhood, been fascinated by cities lost to human memory—places that had to be dug out and reimagined, their stories pieced together from their remains. His first flesh and bone encounters with such 'lost cities' began in his mid-twenties with the ruins of the Mayans and the Aztecs, still partly covered by earth and forest. Since then, he has explored dozens of 'lost cities' across nearly sixty countries. In 2004, he and his life partner, Usha Alexander, left their jobs to travel through India for two years, visiting hundreds of amazing historical and natural sites across twenty states.

Returning to a day job in California, Namit continued to read across academic history, ancient and modern literature, archaeology, anthropology, economics and political thought, seeking to connect the dots across India's complex historical terrain. He engaged with Ambedkarite, feminist and Hindu nationalist thinkers. He missed being in India, but he also felt grateful for his stint abroad, which, among other things, equipped him to more deeply behold India in light of the world. He published travelogues, book reviews, and essays on social and historical themes. His interest in history and travel naturally merged into a form that combined narrative history with archaeological travel writing.

In 2013, Namit and his partner left their Silicon Valley lives and moved back to India to devote themselves to reading and writing. For a couple of years, he volunteered for public interest causes such as clean air and renewable energy, where he led the drafting of the first-ever solar energy policy for Delhi. By now, he had also grown more sensitive to non-elite perspectives of India's past—the 'view from below'—rare in histories written by foreigners and upper-caste Indians, and he wanted to give them more space in his writing. These efforts came together in his first book, *The Lottery of Birth: On Inherited Social Inequalities* (2017), a collection of essays published by Three Essays Collective.

After over three decades of exploring history, Namit began working on *Indians: A Brief History of a Civilization*, which was published by Penguin Random House India in 2021. In 2024, he wrote and anchored a ten-part history web series based substantially on this book and bearing the same name. He will soon resume work on a 'sequel', provisionally titled *Modern Indians.* (He has also come to see this author bio as an amusingly quaint exercise in writing stylized prose about oneself in the third person.)

§

www.ingramcontent.com/pod-product-compliance
Ingram Content Group UK Ltd
Pitfield, Milton Keynes, MK11 3LW, UK
UKHW021402190726
13845UKWH00028B/834

9 789383 968473